This beautifully written book will be invaluable to any techno
to develop the soft skills that are so important to make a di
workplace. Easy to read with warmth and wisdom, and ill
examples, I highly recommend it.

I0050688

Simon Marvell,
Founder and Director, Acuity Risk Management Limited

IT permeates every facet of modern life. Yet often, even with the best intentions, the rationale for technical decisions is not always explained in a way that is of value to users. This book is a practical 'how to' guide for every technologist where they can learn to understand their audience and apply certain methodologies to constructively develop these key skills. It brings together a range of real world examples, research and tools for effective communication. Highly recommended.

Amanda Annandale,
Business Architect, KPMG LLP

It's great to see another practical resource covering the soft skills needed to be successful in information technology. This isn't a textbook, it's peppered with anecdotes and advice borne from real world experience. The book covers a range of practical tools, tips and techniques across a number of key areas such as knowing your audience, storytelling and how to collaborate allowing you to build trust with the teams around you and become an effective part of the wider team.

Alex Woodward CITP,
VP UK Cyber, CGI

Mastering Communication and Collaboration is a refreshingly bold and captivating read. I found the exploration of storytelling's influence on teamwork and simplifying intricate workplace matters particularly intriguing. This book truly spotlights the undervalued skill of using narratives to forge connections, making it a standout aspect of its content.

Ian Murphy,
Founder, CyberOff

An enjoyable read, which articulates the points of communication and collaboration really well with good everyday working examples. I would recommend this book for all levels of experience and this topic is very key in this new age of hybrid working.

Ranjit Attalia,
Senior Business Analysis, Financial Conduct Authority

Mastering Communication and Collaboration is a thought-provoking publication that applies insight to those wishing to review and improve their communication skills to collaborate effectively. Whilst the content is relevant to all modes of working, the ideas are particularly timely given the rise in home working and the need to use tools to communicate remotely.

John Burns LL.M, CEng, MBCS,
Information Security Risk Analyst

This book is the ultimate guide for IT professionals seeking to excel in teamwork and leadership. With insightful chapters on communication, data presentation, emotional intelligence, and more, this book is a game-changer for those aiming to thrive in the tech world. Its comprehensive approach equips readers with the essential skills needed to navigate the complex and dynamic IT landscape with finesse.

Rishikesh Yardi,
Product Leader

MASTERING COMMUNICATION AND COLLABORATION

BCS, THE CHARTERED INSTITUTE FOR IT

BCS, The Chartered Institute for IT, is committed to making IT good for society. We use the power of our network to bring about positive, tangible change. We champion the global IT profession and the interests of individuals, engaged in that profession, for the benefit of all.

Exchanging IT expertise and knowledge
The Institute fosters links between experts from industry, academia and business to promote new thinking, education and knowledge sharing.

Supporting practitioners
Through continuing professional development and a series of respected IT qualifications, the Institute seeks to promote professional practice tuned to the demands of business. It provides practical support and information services to its members and volunteer communities around the world.

Setting standards and frameworks
The Institute collaborates with government, industry and relevant bodies to establish good working practices, codes of conduct, skills frameworks and common standards. It also offers a range of consultancy services to employers to help them adopt best practice.

Become a member
Over 70,000 people including students, teachers, professionals and practitioners enjoy the benefits of BCS membership. These include access to an international community, invitations to a roster of local and national events, career development tools and a quarterly thought-leadership magazine. Visit www.bcs.org/membership to find out more.

Further information
BCS, The Chartered Institute for IT,
3 Newbridge Square,
Swindon, SN1 1BY, United Kingdom.
T +44 (0) 1793 417 417
(Monday to Friday, 09:00 to 17:00 UK time)
www.bcs.org/contact
http://shop.bcs.org/

MASTERING COMMUNICATION AND COLLABORATION

A comprehensive guide to teamwork and leadership for IT professionals

By Angus McIlwraith

© BCS Learning and Development Ltd 2023

The right of Angus McIlwraith to be identified as author of this work has been asserted by him in accordance with sections 77 and 78 of the Copyright, Designs and Patents Act 1988.

Published by BCS Learning and Development Ltd, a wholly owned subsidiary of BCS, The Chartered Institute for IT, 3 Newbridge Square, Swindon, SN1 1BY, UK.
www.bcs.org

Paperback ISBN: 978-1-78017-6048
PDF ISBN: 978-1-78017-6055
ePUB ISBN: 978-1-78017-6062

Ebook available

British Cataloguing in Publication Data.
A CIP catalogue record for this book is available at the British Library.

Publisher's acknowledgements
Reviewers: Katie Walsh and Jill Shepherd
Publisher: Ian Borthwick
Sales director: Charles Rumball
Commissioning editor: Heather Wood
Production manager: Florence Leroy
Project manager: Sunrise Setting Ltd
Copy-editor: Sarah Cook
Proofreader: Barbara Eastman
Indexer: David Gaskell
Cover design: Alex Wright
Cover image: iStock-AscentXmedia
Typeset by Lapiz Digital Services, Chennai, India

CONTENTS

LIST OF FIGURES AND TABLES

AUTHOR

Angus McIlwraith has worked in information security since 1984 primarily as a consultant. Something he regularly encounters is the need to develop, implement and maintain good communication and collaboration skills. It's easy to forget that sometimes you must explain yourself to people who don't have your background, skills or training. Angus has produced multi-media material providing culture change, awareness improvement and resilience testing, and written for many professional magazines, provided business guidance for small and medium-sized enterprises (SMEs) on UK government websites, developed and assessed training courses under the GCHQ Certified Training (GCT) scheme, and delivered material for BCS professional and apprenticeship qualifications.

NOTE FROM THE AUTHOR

My professional experience has been primarily in the field of information security. This is a broad church and encompasses many facets – IT being not the least of them. I have argued for many years that one of the key failings of the information security profession has been a failure to understand its true purpose and to communicate this effectively with non-specialists. The introduction to a book I published in 2006[1] contained the following passage:

> The manner in which information security has been presented by the media has been, and remains, poor – perhaps understandably so in that journalists are by nature generalists and have to relate complex issues rapidly and succinctly. Some of the blame for this misrepresentation has to lie squarely within the information security profession itself.

I held the heart-felt belief that this state of affairs would change, but I am constantly reminded that there is an area of professional life that we all (information security people, IT specialists, enterprise architects and all the rest of us) need to address. We all need to ensure we communicate clearly and effectively, and from this, the benefits of fruitful collaboration can flow.

What used to be 'data security' became 'computer security' and evolved into 'information security'. The change in emphasis from 'information security' to 'cyber security' in recent years has perhaps put the clock back somewhat. It seems there is a regression away from a business-oriented approach to a technical mindset that is introspective and insular. I recently had a notification in the timeline of my LinkedIn profile that had a questionnaire that asked the following:

What is the primary goal of cybersecurity?

- *Protecting computer hardware*
- *Securing network connections*
- *Preventing unauthorized access*
- *Encrypting data*

---

1 McIlwraith, A. (2006) *Information Security and Employee Behaviour: How to Reduce Risk Through Employee Education, Training and Awareness.* Aldershot, UK: Gower.

I was unable to respond meaningfully because none of the options were, in my opinion, primary. They are all facets of higher-level goals, which could be:

- 'to ensure the resilience of an organisation's processes'; or
- 'to preserve the confidentiality, integrity and availability of the information an organisation handles'.

We could achieve either of the above by (amongst many other things) protecting computer hardware, securing network connections, preventing unauthorised access and encrypting data. Cyber security too often operates 'in the weeds'. We need to get our heads up and see the bigger picture **and** make sure we understand what the weeds are up to. Many parts of this book deal with self-perception. If we information professionals cannot engage those areas of thinking that allow us to see ourselves as others see us, we will be less effective in all aspects of our work. A narrow focus on specific skill sets and a narrow understanding of the needs of others is not a good mix. There are schools of thought and multiple sources of knowledge and wisdom that we ignore at our peril.

In this book I make reference to a wide range of sources. Some are academic, others are political or managerial. I also use a lot of ancient sources. This is not to demonstrate the depth and breadth of my education and knowledge,[2] but to make a simple point. The point is that in almost all circumstances, there is nothing new under the sun. The Greeks had a word for most things. Ancient cultures still have the ability to teach, inspire and admonish us in equal measure.

This book is aimed primarily at IT professionals, but I'm confident people who work in other specialisms will recognise some of the tenets and examples used and can make use of what I hope is useful learning. Specialists only become truly effective when they recognise and can empathise with the needs of others. That's what this book is really about – helping people become and remain effective.

---

[2]   I actually have a GCE O Level in Ancient Greek – my only formal language qualification. λυώ τους δούλούς.

ABBREVIATIONS

2FA	two-factor authentication
AI	artificial intelligence
CBT	cognitive behavioural therapy
C&C	command and control
CompTIA	Computing Technology Industry Association
EI	emotional intelligence
GCT	GCHQ Certified Training
GDPR	General Data Protection Regulation
HR	human resources
IT	information technology
KAB	knowledge, attitude and behaviour
MS	Microsoft
NHS	National Health Service
ONS	Office for National Statistics (UK)
PDSA	Deming Cycle Plan, Do, Study, Act
PII	personally identifiable information
PMA	positive mental attitude
PR	public relations
RCA	root cause analysis
SBI	Situation, Behaviour and Impact
SCORM	Shareable Content Object Reference Model
SMART	specific, measurable, achievable, relevant and time-bound
STAR	Situation, Task, Action and Result
TBO	the bleeding obvious
TNA	training needs analysis
USCB	United States Census Bureau

INTRODUCTION

BACKGROUND

This book came about from a conversation I had with a member of one of BCS' management teams responsible for developing and delivering various vocational courses for their membership. I had helped develop parts of the syllabus for one such course, and when looking at the final version I was struck by an immediate impression – the syllabus looked like the table of contents for a hopefully interesting and useful book. They suggested I put forward a proposal, and after being pushed back a couple of times, we agreed to proceed. The syllabus is firmly focused on IT practitioners from disciplines including testing, architecture and governance. You may notice that many examples and analogies I use emerge from my own specialism – information security. I have tried to make sure that they are of relevance to all IT practitioners – I'm convinced they are.

Any reader needs to know 'what's in it for me?' before choosing to read a book. As the original table of contents was based on the syllabus of the BCS IT Business Partner course, the content is intended to support learning and understanding of that syllabus, and help readers achieve the qualification. It is **not** a textbook – its intention is to provide knowledge, insights and understanding of communication and collaboration for technical people working in IT and related professions. It is also intended to be informative and (hopefully) entertaining.

Whatever school or specialism you come from, with digital transformation at the forefront of many organisational strategies, there is an ever-growing need for IT professionals to be equipped with rounded business knowledge and robust interpersonal and leadership skills. BCS have developed a series of syllabi designed to meet this need. These include:

- Business Skills for the Digital Professional;
- Collaborating with Business Teams;
- Leading with a Digital Mindset;
- Being an IT Business Partner.

This book provides material that covers the subject matter set out in the 'Collaborating with Business Teams' syllabus. It also seeks to enhance your (the reader) understanding by providing case studies, analogies, examples and stories. It draws on experience and tales from many places, industries and sectors. It also provides a degree of historical and cultural context. Many issues we meet today are not new and can be better understood if seen from a range of angles and perspectives. For example, if any more mature readers are ever tempted to lament the quality of today's youth, or if you are younger and feel that the previous generation is being overly critical, read the following:

> Young people are high-minded because they have not yet been humbled by life, nor have they experienced the force of circumstances... They think they know everything and are always quite sure about it. (Aristotle – 4th century BCE)

I think that the need for the digital partnering approach is very clear – it's been needed for some time, and there have been initiatives to look at the root problem. In 1983 I was given the opportunity to study for an MSc degree in Information Technology at what was then Brighton Polytechnic (now the University of Brighton). It was the first intake on the first course of its kind, in that it sought to take non-IT and non-science graduates and mould them into effective technology practitioners. There was at the time a shortage of technologists (nothing new there then) and this was an attempt (funded centrally by the UK government) to help alleviate this. It was also thought that it might be easier to teach technology to liberal-arts graduates than to teach outright technologists how to talk and write in a way so that normal people could understand them.

The degree course approach was novel, but it's clear to me that the issue the course sought to alleviate has not been resolved. There remains a gap after these many years. This is probably a terribly generalised statement, but many people in IT are extremely knowledgeable, skilled and capable in their core subject matter – but remain less so in regard to how best to operate in the organisations within which they work. For people to be effective and generate value for their organisation, it is essential that this gap is filled.

This is the purpose of the BCS syllabus-based training courses – to help people to become IT business partners – and this book seeks, amongst other things, to support those attempting the courses. The book can also be read and used as a stand-alone publication – it is meant to aid anybody trying to improve the way they operate, be they in the private sector, government or elsewhere.

WHAT IS AN IT BUSINESS PARTNER?

It's very apparent that the 2020/2021 COVID-19 pandemic increased focus across all sectors on digital skills and digital transformation. Increased adoption of digital technologies and digital transformation attracts increasing attention and priority. Digital skills are increasingly critical across all sectors. What is also emerging is a realisation that IT and digital technology need not be seen as a cost centre. IT deployment that is well-executed is a driver of profit rather than a cost. Technical people need to ensure this remains the case and engage with the organisational core and form a true partnership with overall objectives.

WorldSkills UK is an independent charity that works with employers, education and governments in the UK. It is a member of WorldSkills, a global initiative that supports young people through competitions-based training, assessment, and benchmarking. In 2021 they published their *Disconnected* report[3] that analysed the UK's digital skills

---

3 See https://www.worldskillsuk.org/wp-content/uploads/2021/03/Disconnected-Report-final.pdf.

market. It emerged that 60 per cent of businesses believe their reliance on advanced digital skills will increase over the next five years. However, only 48 per cent believed that young people are leaving full-time education with sufficient advanced digital skills.

As was apparent in 1983 (see above earlier reference to the Brighton University MSc degree in Information Technology), demand for digital talent and skills is still outstripping supply.

Role definition

There is no single definition of what an IT business partner is. I performed a high-level qualitative analysis of a range of job descriptions to crystallise a reasonable understanding of the relevant skills and knowledge required for the role. The following bullets set out the results of this analysis:

- a 'trusted technology advisor to the customer to ensure that technology delivery and service aligns to the business strategy and operational requirements. As an IT business partner you will be responsible for developing and delivering a digital strategy and a roadmap for your customer';
- a 'trusted advisor' – the primary IT point of contact to business line executives and managers;
- proactive and anticipatory in their thinking;
- an essential conduit and support service for information about digital technology around the entire organisation;
- helps to resolve technology-related queries and gains a clear understanding of where assistance and communication is required;
- eyes and ears of the IT department.

Recurring terms include:

- identifying opportunities;
- providing an interface;
- generating business value;
- delivering the strategic, creative and technical development of digital products;
- understanding market challenges;
- tracking and communicating information;
- promoting IT services and capabilities;
- enabling the business to achieve their objectives through the effective use of technology.

Having core IT skills is a given – an IT business partner cannot operate without these – but it's obvious from the phrases and terms listed above that the route to becoming effective is business awareness, communication, empathy and listening. The skills and insights set out in the following chapters form a model for the kind of communication and collaboration skills required of the IT business partner role. What is important is to realise that the skills required for an IT business partner are as valid for anyone operating in any technical or specialist area. They are not confined to the specific role and will provide value to anyone. What is also important to note is that the prime driver behind the role (and therefore the skills required) is to add business value. Improved communication and collaboration should help organisations to make money, and save money – preferably both.

Soft skills

The concept of the IT business partner is not new, and it is appropriate at this time to firstly focus on the terms 'hard' and 'soft' skills. Soft skills are those much sought after personal qualities that are not normally gained through formal training. They include common sense, the ability to get on with people, and having a positive flexible attitude. Many people of a technical persuasion place great emphasis on the so-called 'hard skills' and dismiss the 'soft' as peripheral and somehow less relevant. In 1918, the Carnegie Foundation undertook research into how important various skill types were to become a successful engineer.[4] The results were stark – 85 per cent of job success comes from having well-developed soft skills, and only 15 per cent from technical skills and knowledge. Ongoing research shows that this ratio has changed little in the intervening 100 years, and that our education and training regimes in schools and colleges have failed to react to this.[5] What is very apparent is that these so-called 'soft' skills can be learned and can be improved through experience and practice. More detail on this report is provided in the Appendix 'Carnegie Foundation'.

One of the possible reasons why soft skills are treated so oddly (given their obvious importance) relates to how people try to measure things and handle the resulting metrics. Many metrics are taken up and used for one simple reason – they are easy to collect. Measuring capability in technical subject matter (part of 'hard skills') is easier than measuring capability in soft skills such as empathy. This is perhaps one of the reasons it doesn't get taught in any meaningfully formal manner – because it's hard to quantify and grade.

Most people have an innate need for certainty, and this is one of the reasons why easily gathered metrics can provide some comfort. This phenomenon is amplified by the media who constantly seek definite numbers – such as NHS waiting list times, the numbers of people accepted for immigration and so on. Dealing with uncertainty takes many people into what they think is psychologically unsafe ground.

What is very apparent is that soft skills relate to **how** you work. They go beyond empathy and include:

- adaptability;
- communication;
- compromise;

---

4   Mann, C.R. (1918) A study of engineering education, Bulletin No 11. The Carnegie Foundation for the Advancement of Teaching.

5   Green, M. and McGill, E. (2011) The State of the Industry Report. American Society for Training and Development (ASTD).

- conflict resolution;
- creative thinking;
- critical thinking;
- dependability;
- leadership;
- listening;
- motivation;
- negotiation;
- positivity;
- problem solving;
- teamwork;
- time management.

The list above is an amalgam of research covering a range of sources, including recruitment agencies, the US Department of Labor, respected business publications and academic courses. What is also very apparent is that they are amongst the most sought-after skills by employers. This is because the skills help people to become adaptable and flexible – characteristics that are becoming increasingly important when organisations use Agile approaches to project management and system development. They are also essential once you grow into managerial roles, as the need for clear collaboration and communication become key.

For example, the 2018 Financial Times MBA Skills Gap survey[6] was very clear. Businesses value the ability to work in a team. They value the ability to work with a wide range of people, and to build, sustain and expand a network of valuable contacts. It is perhaps counter-intuitive that the least valued skills identified in the survey included accounting, programming and economics. Businesses value collaboration. Note that the survey also indicated that the soft skills are harder to find and are considered harder to attain and use than the more commonly taught 'hard-skills'. This trend is not going to go away – I will return to it constantly. The findings of the 2018 survey are repeated across many more recent studies. The report 'Closing the skills gap 2023: employer perspectives on educating the post-pandemic workforce' by Wiley[7] repeats and amplifies the same findings.

Perception, innumeracy and human nature

Measuring the value and impact of the so-called 'soft skills' is difficult, and this is one of the main reasons why they are not managed in the same way as 'hard skills' are. They are hard to measure empirically, and there are other seemingly less empirical impediments to enabling sound collaboration and communication – not least as regards

---

6 *Financial Times*. What top employers want from MBA graduates. https://www.ft.com/content/64b19e8e-aaa5-11e8-89a1-e5de165fa619.

7 Capranos, D. and Magda, A.J. (2023) Closing the skills gap 2023: employer perspectives on educating the post-pandemic workforce. Maitland, FL: Wiley.

how many things are perceived. There is a move to change this approach that may impact positively on this. The Spotify HR Blog[8] states the following:

> Soft gives the impression that the skill is soft as in weak or fuzzy, versus the hard skill being strong, clear and indisputable. It can also be hard to actually agree on what skills fit into the hard vs soft category.

The blog suggests a move to the use of the terms 'durable' and 'perishable' skills. The blog continues:

> Using these names removes the implicit bias and reduces the fuzzy line or question marks of which category a skill belongs to. And it takes into account the longevity of different skills.

Perishable skills typically have a lifespan of less than two and a half years. Examples include operating system platform expertise, specialist programming languages – anything that tends to operate dynamically. Durable skills are transferable and rarely connected to a specific role. They tend to remain valid for longer timeframes – up to eight years, and include communication, collaboration, leadership and so forth.

Becoming a sound collaborator and communicator is not restricted to your direct communication abilities. You must also understand how you are perceived and through this, how your communications might be interpreted. There are later sections in this book that cover some specifics on **how** to communicate and collaborate. This section provides some grounding in understanding how numbers are used to demonstrate a point and impact on risk perception.

Many people do not understand numbers well, and often make decisions based on what is superficially logical. However, the merest touch of analysis often reveals truths that are less seemingly intuitive.

When the UK National Identity Card was first mooted and then delivered, there were changes introduced into the way people in the UK could apply for ID cards and passports. The ID card initiative was scrapped in 2011. These changes involved setting up many offices across the UK that were used to interview applicants. This was part of a range of measures designed to reduce fraud in the application process. It was expensive and time-consuming, and as such was inevitably open to scrutiny and criticism. One very senior political leader asked a question – 'How many criminals have you detected by carrying out these interviews?' The answer was clear – none. This was used to denigrate the process as failing to catch wrongdoers. The accusation was flawed due to one simple issue – the process was not designed to catch criminals. It was designed to stop criminals getting hold of valuable identity documents. One key point of the process was deterrence. It's very hard to provide metrics for a process that has potentially stopped something happening. How do you measure something that hasn't happened?

---

8   See https://hrblog.spotify.com/2022/03/18/categorizing-skills-more-than-just-semantics/.

This factor really comes into play when dealing with some abstract concepts such as risk (with its attendant subject matter that includes likelihood and probability). People have an inbuilt tendency to personalise events, and this overrides fact-based statistics (including risk estimates). People also tend to engage in what is known as selective filtering of information and tend to come to spurious conclusions. If you ever try to use statistics to present a case, you will have to bear this in mind. There are many examples of how risk is perceived that do not tally with reality. In the US, you are more likely to be shot by a toddler than by a terrorist.

Examples of personalising events are many. Work undertaken by Fischhoff, Slovic and Lichtenstein[9] established that if events are thought of as being external or foreign, they are considered riskier than something familiar or internal (see Table I.1). This is why information security practitioners pursue 'hackers', foreign intelligence services and organised criminals with far more vigour than they manage internal threats – such as seemingly loyal, long-serving staff members. It is the latter that are far more likely to cause a problem. You have to be aware of this tendency to view the world in a way that is distorted by this issue

Table I.1 Risk perception (Source: Sandman, P.M. (no date) *Explaining environmental risk*. Available from https://www.psandman.com/articles/explain3.htm)

Less risky	More risky
Chronic	Acute
Controllable	Uncontrollable
Controlled by self	Controlled by others
Detectable	Undetectable
Diffuse in time and space	Focused in time and space
Fair	Unfair
Familiar	Unfamiliar
Immediate	Delayed
Natural	Artificial
Voluntary	Involuntary

People have a plethora of inbuilt prejudices that have to be borne in mind when trying to change their minds through collaboration and communication. I have a personal example of my own prejudice that emerged during employment in local government.

---

9 Fischhoff, B., Slovic, P. and Lichtenstein, S. (1979) Weighing the risks: risks: benefits which risks are acceptable? *Environment: Science and Policy for Sustainable Development*, 21 (4). 17–38.

Another example of familiarity impacting on how security is managed is the way in which security managers perceive local levels of threat and risk. Many years ago, I worked for about 18 months in the housing department of a city council. My job involved the collection of rent arrears, and continued non-payment sometimes culminated in the eviction of tenants. One of the senior managers asked me one day what percentage of tenants I thought were in arrears with their rent. I suggested about 15 per cent. The actual figure was 2 per cent (amongst the best in the UK at the time). My close involvement with the matter had caused me to internally exaggerate the numbers. For the same reason, information security managers see hackers on every corner. This phenomenon relates to the need to decrease controls once a threat has passed or when the initial reaction to a threat is seen as being excessive.[10]

As to how you are perceived, it is also fair to say that many people perceive IT and its related practices (such as cyber security) with a degree of caution. We have already established that the role of the IT business partner is to help ensure IT is a key enabler for the organisation. You must always ensure you let people know what the benefits are. You must present the upside and navigate the complexities of how risks, numbers and perception can work against you.

Money, metrics and markets

As a closing section for the Introduction of this book, for anyone with aspirations to work as an IT business partner, there are broader aspects outside the immediate scope that need to be considered – many of them are covered in other BCS syllabi. Remember that knowing and understanding how your collaboration and communication skills fit into the broader scheme of things will make you more effective. For example, love it or hate it, money matters. Knowing how budgets work will help you to shape decisions and help to make requesting funding easier. The beauty and effectiveness of your brilliant communications won't always be obvious to others. It must be seen in terms and metrics other people understand – and money is undoubtably a universal and very powerful metric. Ideas must be communicated in a manner that meets the needs of the audience, using terms and examples that they recognise and understand.

Once your brilliant idea has been accepted, it must be created, developed and implemented. A friend of mine was responsible for setting up a company that provided anti-malware services across the internet. It was successful, but he told me once with great earnestness that 'there is nothing more difficult that I know of than bringing a new idea to market'. This is where leadership comes in. Bringing something to market requires us to drive change. The problem has been known about for years:

It must be considered that there is nothing more difficult to carry out, nor more doubtful of success, nor dangerous to handle, than to initiate a new order of things.

---

10 McIlwraith, A. (2006) *Information Security and Employee Behaviour: How to Reduce Risk Through Employee Education, Training and Awareness*. Aldershot, UK: Gower.

For the reformer has enemies and only lukewarm defenders. He must confront the disbelief of mankind, who do not truly believe in anything new until they actually experience it. (From *The Prince* by Niccolo di Bernardo dei Machiavelli (1469–1527))

You will need to know your ground and have business skills. You will have to learn to communicate and collaborate. You will have to provide leadership.

Very few people are entirely technical but unable to talk to non-specialists. Very few people are completely technically ignorant but able to talk the leaves from the trees. Most of us exist in a spectrum between these two extremes. This book seeks to find that common ground that may in some way help us all.

1 COMMUNICATION – PARADOX, PURPOSE AND INTENTION

The word 'paradox' in the title refers to the fact that, in most circumstances, communication and collaboration require you to work in two ways simultaneously. Firstly, you must avoid patronising your audience (be they readership, or listeners, or viewers) by talking down to them, whilst at the same time ensuring you don't drift into jargon or other specialist means of excluding members of your audience. The theme of the paradox will be repeated throughout this book. This leads me into my first dilemma – I am going to ask what might seem a potentially patronising question – it being 'Why communicate?' It might seem completely obvious and intuitive, but there's nothing like a bit of empirical data to back up such intuitive and obvious claims or hunches.

THE PURPOSE AND INTENTION OF COMMUNICATION

In 2007, the Computing Technology Industry Association (CompTIA) undertook a survey to investigate what were the primary causes of IT project failure. More than 1,000 people responded, with almost 28 per cent stating that poor communication was the number one cause of project failure. Insufficient resource planning was the second cause, scoring slightly less than 18 per cent. Unrealistic deadlines were the third listed cause – scoring 13 per cent.

Communication is not just about style of delivery. In a project management context, it requires the communicator to understand the matter in hand, which must include such things as project objectives, potential results and budget limitations. They must also consider the 'audience', and they must consider the medium they use for communication.

Poor communication is not limited to the worlds of IT and business. Academia is riddled with the same malaise. One of my favourites is this example from a book by Barbara Vinken named *Flaubert Postsecular: Modernity Crossed Out*:

> The work of the text is to literalize the signifiers of the first encounter, dismantling the ideal as an idol. In this literalization, the idolatrous deception of the first moment becomes readable. The ideal will reveal itself to be an idol. Step by step, the ideal is pursued by a devouring doppelganger, tearing apart all transcendence. This de-idealization follows the path of reification, or, to invoke Augustine, the path of carnalization of the spiritual. Rhetorically, this is effected through literalization. A Sentimental Education does little more than elaborate the progressive literalization of the Annunciation.[11]

---

11 Vinken, B. (2015) *Flaubert Postsecular: Modernity Crossed Out*. Stanford: Stanford University Press.

I read a couple of online synopses of the book in an attempt to understand what the paragraph above might mean. I couldn't understand the synopses either.

I am not alone in holding such poor communication in contempt. The Canadian-American cognitive psychologist Steven Pinker wrote a wonderful article called 'Why academics stink at writing'. He states:

> Bad writing is a deliberate choice. Scholars in the softer[12] fields spout obscure verbiage to hide the fact that they have nothing to say. They dress up the trivial and obvious with the trappings of scientific sophistication, hoping to bamboozle their audiences with highfalutin gobbledygook.[13]

The reasons for such professional narcissism can include what Pinker calls 'hedging language' with phrases such as 'so to speak', 'to a certain degree', 'to some extent' and 'I would argue' used in order for authors to distance themselves from the claims they are making in their text just in case their evidence is not conclusive.

One of the more eloquently analysed examples of poor technical communication centres on a near-catastrophic accident at the Three Mile Island nuclear power plant in 1979. The accident was a partial meltdown of one of the reactors. The eloquent analysis was provided by Pete Sandman, who produced a powerful statement:

> It is still possible for communicators to make the learning easier or harder – and scientists and bureaucrats have acquired a fairly consistent reputation for making it harder. At Three Mile Island, for example, the level of technical jargon was actually higher when the experts were talking to the public and the news media than when they were talking to each other. The transcripts of urgent telephone conversations between nuclear engineers were usually simpler to understand than the transcripts of news conferences. To be sure, jargon is a genuine tool of professional communication, conveying meaning (to those with the requisite training) precisely and concisely. But it also serves as a tool to avoid communication with outsiders, and as a sort of membership badge, a sign of the status difference between the professional and everyone else.[14]

The impact of Three Mile Island is dwarfed by later episodes – most notably the Chernobyl disaster that occurred in 1986 and the 2011 Fukushima nuclear disaster in Japan – but neither have been subjected to the degree of analysis of the communications involved as Three Mile Island.

---

12 Interesting reference of the word 'soft' – a bit like an engineer's distaste for 'soft skills'?

13 Pinker, S. (2022) *Why academics stink at writing-and how to fix it.* The Chronicle of Higher Education. Available from https://www.chronicle.com/article/why-academics-stink-at-writing-and-how-to-fix-it/.

14 Sandman, P.M. (no date) *Explaining environmental risk: dealing with the public.* Peter M. Sandman website. Available from https://www.psandman.com/articles/explain3.htm.

IT, like all specialisms, has its jargon. As Sandman states – it's a 'genuine tool' – but few IT professionals are trained in communication, and many have a well-deserved reputation for being hard to understand and, therefore, difficult to work with. Whilst not everyone is going to operate in potentially catastrophic industries, being capable of clear, concise communication that aids collaboration, assists in getting things right first time, allows non-specialists to understand you, and helps to align your work with broader directives and strategies, is to everyone's benefit. It makes you more effective. It saves time. It saves money. Jargon and specialist terms – particularly acronyms – have their place, in that it is a useful professional communications tool, but misuse is almost always counter-productive. If you are going to use jargon (and it's often sensible to do so), define it up front when you first use it. Sometimes it's worth repeating the exercise at a number of points in the text, and making sure the term appears in a glossary or similar.

It's important to make sure that complex elements – including jargon – are made clear. The closer to simplicity you can get, the more persuasive your content should be. The seemingly growing amount of conspiracy theories, misinformation and 'alternative facts' (aka fake news) are indicative of a reaction by people not understanding things – particularly complicated things. There is an innate need felt by many people for simple explanations – looking for straightforward cause and effect explanations. This has manifested with many people having a related innate distrust of 'experts'[15] and will focus on any poor communication on your part as a reason to ignore, circumvent or belittle you and any case or argument you present.

Richard Portes stated in May 2017:

> More generally, distrust has been encouraged by those who have vested interests in discrediting experts because they want to advance a particular agenda – be that in the field of economics, climate change, health or whatever – which may conflict with what expert opinion would be.[16]

This matter has broad social and political undertones that are more complex than someone being ignorant or suchlike – distrust of authority is bound up with this matter. It is an aspect of life that has been exploited by many unscrupulous people. There is a strong psychological need to seek 'peace of mind'. This manifests in many ways, but one behaviour that is common is ignoring information that makes you feel uncomfortable. This process can be done subconsciously without the need for a deliberate decision. Ignoring facts and opinions that make one feel uncomfortable drives many to avoid following logic and acting solely in an emotional manner. This won't be the last time I mention emotions.

Returning to the work of Steven Pinker, in his book *The Sense of Style: The Thinking Person's Guide to Writing in the 21st Century*,[17] he uses a term that encapsulates a sensible approach when writing – referred to as 'Classic Style'. A classic writer:

- 'counts on the common sense and ordinary charity of his readers'; and

---

15 You only have to undertake brief research on some government pronouncements made concerning Brexit to see this attitude manifest.

16 Portes, R. (2017) *I think the people of this country have had enough of experts*. London Business School. Available from https://www.london.edu/think/who-needs-experts.

17 Pinker, S. (2014) *The Sense of Style: The Thinking Person's Guide to Writing in the 21st Century*. New York: Penguin.

- 'credits the reader with enough intelligence to realize that many concepts aren't easy to define, and that many controversies aren't easy to resolve'.

Pinker also discusses another concept called 'the curse of knowledge'. He states:

> The curse of knowledge is a major reason that good scholars write bad prose. It simply doesn't occur to them that their readers don't know what they know—that those readers haven't mastered the patois or can't divine the missing steps that seem too obvious to mention or have no way to visualize an event that to the writer is as clear as day. And so they don't bother to explain the jargon or spell out the logic or supply the necessary detail.

The two concepts outlined above set out the paradox of relevant, concise, unambiguous and clear communication. You have to be able to count on 'common sense' amongst your readership, yet also ensure that you understand when and how you should explain the 'necessary detail'. You don't want to patronise people, nor do you want to deliver a stream of technobabble. Successful communication relies on your finding the right balance to meet this paradox.

There is so much more to communication than 'good writing'. Meeting the paradox requires you to:

- know your audience;
- understand the best use of delivery channels, methods and tools;
- understand when to communicate, and the frequency of communication;
- understand, interpret and deliver data;
- understand what's data, and what's knowledge;
- be aware of your own skills and limits – especially as regards empathy and emotional intelligence;
- listen;
- understand the power of stories and how to create and deliver them;
- talk to people;
- be flexible and adaptable;
- obtain, listen to and respond to feedback.

The purpose of communication is complex, and highly context dependent. It can pass on a warning. It can express emotion. It can pass on knowledge and wisdom. For the sake of this book, I will limit this 'purpose' to three elements. To educate, to inform and to persuade.

To educate

The key purposes of education are:

- to impart knowledge;

- to improve or develop;
- to train for some particular purpose or occupation.

Knowledge is fundamental, but it is severely hampered and impaired if one does not understand context. The rote learning of facts as an end in itself is rarely of practical use. Improvement and development are about helping someone make best use of their knowledge by providing them with the tools they need to think, and then learn more knowledge – and put it into context. Training provides the tools and techniques by which this virtuous cycle is enacted.

Furthermore, communication does not happen in a vacuum – there must be a reason **why** we are communicating. One of the prime elements of successful communication is understanding its intended outcome. It's almost worth setting an objective based on a question: 'What do I hope to achieve from this communication?' You may want someone to know something. You may want them to understand a concept. You may want to persuade them to adopt a new stance or opinion, or you may wish them to perform a specific act or behave in a particular way. The simple act of asking this question prior to sending an email to a colleague can make it more effective. It may also help by asking 'What do I **not** want to happen when my recipient reads my email?' to make sure you avoid any unintended consequences.

UNINTENDED CONSEQUENCES

Unintended consequences are an inevitable companion to any change process. Many such consequences can be positive – with additional benefits emerging unexpectedly. However, things don't always go this way. In his 2010 book *The Nature of Change or the Law of Unintended Consequences* John Mansfield stated:

> An example of the unexpected results of change is found in the clearing of trees to make available more agricultural land. This practice has led to rising water tables and increasing salinity that eventually reduces the amount of useable land.[18]

Who would have thought that the propellant used in aerosol sprays would damage the Earth's ozone layer? Supposedly 'moral' crusades that focus sex education on abstinence rather than on pragmatic options such as contraception normally leads to an **increase** in teenage pregnancy.

So often there are efforts to promote change using incentives. There is a concept called 'the cobra effect'. A campaign was set up when the UK ruled India to reduce the number of cobra snakes as they were deemed dangerous. They offered

---

18 Mansfield, J. (2010) *The Nature of Change or the Law of Unintended Consequences: An Introductory Text to Designing Complex Systems and Managing Change.* London: Imperial College Press. 4.

payment to anyone who produced the corpses of dead cobras. The approach was initially successful, but people spotted an opportunity. They began to breed cobras with the sole intention of monetary gain. Eventually the authorities realised their error and scrapped the incentive scheme. The snake breeders, realising that their 'stock' was now worthless, released them, thereby massively increasing the overall population of cobras – the exact opposite result of that intended. It's worth looking at Campbell's Law[19] (the more any quantitative social indicator is used for social decision making the more subject it will be to corruption pressures and the more apt it will be to distort and corrupt the social processes it is intended to monitor) and Goodhart's Law[20] (when a measure becomes a target, it ceases to be a good measure) for more information on this phenomenon.

If you have an intended outcome, it becomes easier to ensure your communication has been successful. You will have succeeded if your intended outcome has happened, and that there have been no undesirable, unintended consequences. Whatever your intention, assessing the possible unintended consequences and their likelihood can save you a world of pain.

Setting objectives is normally part of broader schemes such as education programmes and training courses. However, it does not hurt to use this simple approach during everyday activities such as sending messages or making a phone call. It's also nice to know when you have actually achieved what you set out to do – even on such a microscopic scale. We will return to the matter of objectives and measuring success in more detail in later chapters.

To inform

Informing means telling people something – letting them know. To inform someone means you are providing information to others to help them understand something that you understand, and will help them make informed, rational decisions. You are giving them knowledge (more on this later).

A random stream of facts rarely passes information on – you need to break it down into pieces that have context and can essentially be digested in real time. The use of allegory, metaphors and examples helps to make the facts easier to assimilate. Use simple language, avoid technical complexity and avoid terms not used in the social context you are in. Use straightforward language that people will understand. Avoid technical words, jargon and words that are not commonly understood. Make sure your facts are facts (and not assertions or opinions).

---

19 Campbell, D.T. (1979) Assessing the impact of planned social change. *Evaluation and Program Planning*, 2 (1). 67–90.

20 Goodhart, C. (1975) Problems of monetary management: the U.K. experience. In Courakis, Anthony S. (ed.). *Inflation, Depression, and Economic Policy in the West*. Totowa, NJ: Barnes & Noble (published 1981). 116.

To persuade

Persuasion is one of the key concepts that this book seeks to support. Most of the techniques set out in all the chapters link strongly to the aim of getting people to do things in the manner you want them to do it. The American psychologist Kenneth Berrien identified four concepts that form part of a model for persuasion.[21] In this model, four negotiation approaches exist:

- emotion;
- logic;
- bargaining;
- compromise.

What is key is that in his model Berrien also connected with the concept of emotional intelligence. He also included the aspects of intuition and influence into his model. There are many ways in which persuasion can be studied or investigated, but I'm primarily concerned with looking at persuasion in regard to influencing peoples' attitude or behaviour towards an idea or concept by using written or audio-visual means to convey information, feelings or reasoning, or a combination of all these things.

Persuasion is not always used for benevolent purposes. It can be used for selfish personal gain. It can be used to promote violence or convince people to take a discriminatory viewpoint against minorities. Many such uses of persuasion use the darker side of the palette – aggressive coercion and indoctrination through propaganda. I discount these as they have no place in a civilised society. See 'Communication intention' in Chapter 6 for more details on this.

In Berrien's model, emotion is the trait that relates most closely to the 'emotional intelligence' concept discussed in detail in Chapter 11. Operating at an emotional level requires you to both understand (and to an extent, control) your own emotional state, as well as being able 'read' another person. It operates in a manner that sometimes defies logic and can confuse people who seek to use **logic** as their primary means to persuade people (see below).

It can be argued that the approaches used in the pre-referendum debates on Brexit in the UK revealed an emotional approach by the 'Leave' campaign – touting non-specific attributes such as 'sovereignty' and 'freedom' in a way that appealed to the emotions of many of the electorate. The imagery used was powerful, leveraging concepts such as 'patriotism' to convince people of the correctness of a vote to Leave. The logic employed by many of the 'Remain' faction talked in cold terms regarding trade losses and similar economic harm, or delays at borders for travellers. It could be argued that emotion won because the Remain camp was conceited and forgot that many people respond with their gut instinct rather than by ingesting cold, hard facts. The Leave faction's use of the emotive term 'project fear' to describe the messages from the Remain camp is another example of the use of emotive terms and means.

---

21 Berrien, K. (1944) *Practical Psychology*. New York: Macmillan.

Logical persuasion relies almost entirely on above-said cold facts, figures and precise rationality. It often uses the IT-related Boolean approach of logical operators such as AND, OR, NOT, NOR, NAND and XOR. The answer to a question falls off the end of a series of logical steps, with clear yes/no or true/false cases that lead to a single, logical conclusion. Oh, were it that simple. It does not account for the strange, illogical thing known as a person. Emotion clouds the logic. If you are seeking to persuade someone to change the way they do things, you have to factor in **both** aspects. People often actively rebel against facts (remember the quote 'I think we've all had enough of experts' stated by a prominent political member of the Brexit 'Leave' faction). Logic can be perceived as patronising and intrusive.

Bargaining is a technique that combines both the emotive and logical aspects of persuasion, wherein you have to ensure you get what you want by convincing another person that what you're offering gives them what they want. A key question you can use when attempting to strike a bargain operates at both the emotional and logical levels is, 'what's in it for me?' Whilst retaining the logical approach of ensuring you don't drive a bargain against yourself, you have to ask the question from your opposite number's viewpoint (there's a little bit of emotional intelligence for you). To convince someone that something (a change of heart or mind) is in **their** interest. You can agree that you're seeking something in your own interests, but without reciprocity, it's very hard to change someone's mind or behaviour.

Central to bargaining is the use of compromise. Sometimes you have to give things away to get what you want. I've written many business proposals that contain elements that can be best described as 'sacrificial'.[22] They are those things you know you are unlikely to achieve and are happy to surrender. This gives your opposite number the chance to obtain a 'win' – an important psychological boost that you can exploit for your own ends, in that if people think they've gained an advantage or a concession, they are more likely to strike a bargain in short order. The trick is to try and only concede those things you don't need.

CONCLUSION

I suggest that the core purpose of communication is to persuade people to do things in a manner of **your** choosing. As with initiatives as diverse as marketing campaigns for a new soap powder to information security education and awareness programmes, the core element remains persuasion.

Marketing often uses the acronym KAB (knowledge, attitude and behaviour) to describe what you need to **know** to succeed, and what you need to **change**. An individual who obtains knowledge often exhibits a change in attitude. Changes in attitude often result in a change in behaviour. However, it is not a simple mechanical process – these ghastly human beings keep getting in the way and doing things that defy logic. I suggest that

---

22 There is a variation on this approach that can be used when offering up a document for review. Always include a couple of typos or minor technical errors. The reviewer will point these out with glee and return their comments at pace with an air of superiority. You should thank them and then get on with your work without the overburden of a picky reviewer. These 'errors' are known as 'gimmees'. It works really well on auditors too.

your communications should never be designed to create changes in behaviour – they need to help create the conditions wherein such changes in behaviour are more likely. The better the conditions, the more likely you are to succeed. It's up to you to create the conditions. Don't fall into the trap of thinking that logic prevails – there is no mechanical switch operating here. See Chapter 6 on the way climate change is perceived to show how you need to go beyond the Boolean to succeed.

The links to the skills and knowledge required in marketing in respect of persuading people to do things are clear. You have to look at what you want to achieve and set objectives. This can apply at all levels – even when writing and sending an individual email. What do I want them to do? What are the logical drivers behind my case? What emotional drivers does my intended readership have? You may find you are dealing with a mixed readership and need to ensure you include both logical and emotional elements. You can rarely rely on one – the combined approach covers all bases.

2 KNOW YOUR AUDIENCE

In Chapter 1 I stated that you need to know the purpose of your communication. What effect are you trying to cause? There's an additional element to this – you need to know who you are talking to.

Whilst this statement may fall into that giant bucket termed 'the bleeding obvious' (or TBO for short), it's a consideration that is often **not** considered. The makeup of your audience should have a profound effect on the content of the messages you deliver, how you deliver them, and often, what medium you use to deliver them. It can also dictate how much time you have to pass the messages on. You need to know at what 'level' you need to operate at.

I think it's important to consider some of the terminology that's in common use. The terms 'high-level' and 'low-level' have at least two facets, particularly within the world of IT. There is an implicit snobbery amongst many IT people regarding the use of the 'high-level' programming languages such as Ada, BASIC, COBOL, C, C++, FORTRAN, LISP and the rest. I've known too many IT people disparage these as perhaps relating to 'soft skills'. There is a degree of technical machismo relating to the use of the low-level equivalent – in machine dependent binary or hex. This gap has been further exacerbated by code-generating tools with integrated artificial intelligence (AI) – negating the use of low-level 0s and 1s. The same issues impact on verbal language. I've seen many IT people talk disrespectfully of senior managers (most of whom hold the purse strings) because they do not understand the technical detail and need to be communicated with using non-specialist terms. The reverse is true when senior non-IT specialists complain when people are 'operating down in the weeds'. The whole point of communication is to be heard and understood. If you fail to appreciate and empathise with the needs of your audience and fail to be comprehended, it is **your** fault – not that of your audience.

TECHNICAL SNOBBERY

I overheard a conversation between two highly skilled and deeply experienced information security technical specialists. They were discussing the merits and demerits of various forms of password access control systems. They focused on '2FA' (two-factor authentication), this being the use of stand-alone tokens or mobile phones to increase the security of log-on procedures. They also discussed the use of long, randomly generated passwords – a practice that has been denounced recently by its inventor. During the discussion, one of them mentioned that many people, when they make a mistake when entering a password, have to delete the whole thing and start again. This is because people rely to some degree on muscle-memory when typing in passwords. On hearing this, the listener paused for a few seconds and then said... 'idiots'. This degree of conceit and complacency is the sort of attitude that needs to be eradicated.

Remember – if your communication fails, it's **your** fault. Talking of bad attitude, remember that the only two professional communities that refer to their core customer base as 'users' are IT and the international illegal drugs trade.

The purpose of your communication and the audience determine format and content. Marketing specialists and demographers can provide masses of information and proven techniques for analysing audiences. This is in most instances overkill in the context of this book, but they can be brought to bear.

WHO ARE YOU TALKING TO?

It may sound obvious but you may need to do some research to find out who you are communicating with. You may have the good fortune to be addressing a specific audience without the need for such research, but in many instances you don't have a clue. Sometimes, all you have to do is ask.

A simple approach is to use a simple tool such as a list or a grid. First and foremost, you need to work out what differentiates one type of audience from another. The following bullets can act as a starter:

- position or status within an organisation (perhaps senior, middle and junior management);
- role – core professional (such as a lawyer in a legal practice), administrative or IT for example;
- length of service;
- level of technical knowledge;
- level of engagement;
- location/country;
- language.

Senior management normally require brevity – their time is limited, and they have multiple demands on their diary and attention. Professional specialists often operate within particular vocabulary domains[23] and can tolerate specific jargon and terminology. Long-term employees can understand historic examples, and it's pretty clear that non-native speakers require communication delivered in a way to avoid culturally loaded terms and examples.

---

23 A vocabulary domain is a distinct set of terms used within a specific area of expertise. Lawyers have their own, as do doctors, IT professionals and pigeon fanciers.

WORLD VIEWS, LENSES AND SCHEMAS

Each audience is likely to have a particular world view. Some people use the term 'lens' as a means of illustrating how people can see the same things from a different viewpoint or perspective. A senior manager's 'lens' is likely to differ from the one used by the worker in the loading bay. I tend to look at things through a security lens – causing me to focus on things that a financial accountant would rather avoid. One term I find useful is 'schema'. A schema can be defined as:

- a diagram, plan or scheme;
- an underlying organisational pattern or structure a conceptual framework that provides the basis by which someone relates to the events they experience.

A schema is the world view we all hold in our heads. One particular aspect of such a framework allows us to make rapid decisions. It is based on a primitive survival mechanism that is essentially a model-based approach to thinking. An example of a model-based approach of decision making involves the following logic steps:

The foliage on the bush in front of me is twitching. Foliage doesn't twitch. It might be a leopard. Don't go near the bush!

Our brains are really good at spotting changes in the environment – even if in our heads we simply say 'something has changed here. I'll be wary and try to work out what it is.'

When we examine, even at the most simplistic level, the potential schemas of our possible audiences, it's clear that we need to recognise each of them to some degree. A non-IT senior manager rarely cares one jot about the configuration of a particular router. What they care about is the **impact** a misconfigured router might have in the event of an incident or outage. When dealing with a complex patching problem a software engineer rarely gives significant consideration as to which budget their overtime claims will be made from – provided the problem gets sorted. You need to know what people care about, and what they don't care about.

One of the problems that emerges from such frameworks is that one schema may have truths and logic that contradicts another person's schema's truths and logic. Such truths and logic are often summed up as 'rules of thumb' or heuristics. As is so often the case, there is an ongoing clash between the schemas of cyber security professionals and core business management (especially financial accountants – they hate spending money). The following scenario sets out how this clash can cause unexpected problems.

One of the truths held in the schema of an information security person is that you should never share your log-on password. In many organisations such a practice is commonplace – especially amongst support IT staff as they often need access to such things as privileged user IDs. They may be dealing with an urgent problem, and they need to solve it **now**. Sometimes the only way to do this is by using the equivalent of a Unix root ID. The support team all know each other. They all trust each other. Suddenly some security specialist turns up and tells them they need to establish a regime that involves a PIN-protected safe that contains a single-use password on a slip of paper. The safe can only be opened by two nominated individuals who know one half of the PIN, and who must seek permission from a very senior person within the organisation before proceeding is permitted. Once used, the password has to be changed, the PIN changed and an event log completed. This log has to be signed by just about everybody. The former password sheet has to be cross-shredded in an accredited shredder to a maximum surface area of 6mm^2.

What do you think happens? In many situations you can never find the very senior person required to permit the activity – especially at 3.00 a.m. on a Sunday when they have been attending an especially good dinner party. The nominated individuals will possibly be on leave. Or they may be out on the town. The pragmatic solution is that the IT support people will share the **root** password and keep quiet about it. The clash of the schemas has created problems rather than solving them. This is another example of the concept of 'unintended consequences' mentioned previously.

The security specialist needs to convince the IT support people that protecting **root** is important, and that they need to follow a process. The security specialist needs to understand the likelihood of unexpected consequences. A procedure that works on paper rarely works when it meets reality. It's an old military saying that states 'no plan survives contact with the enemy'. There needs to be flexibility, empathy and, most of all, communication. The security specialist needs to know his audience and needs to provide means that work for the process, rather than making it harder to operate.

JARGON AND MIXED AUDIENCES

It's not just schemas that impact here. The previous chapter talked about jargon – and it's important to understand your audience's level of understanding. What is clear and obvious to an IT support engineer may be jargon-ridden gobbledygook to a marketing manager. The level of abstraction (i.e. the degree to which language is high-level or low-level) required in communication is also important, as is understanding the amount of time a person has to listen to you. If someone does not understand you, in most cases it won't be because they are stupid or ignorant. They know things you don't. Being incomprehensible is **not** a badge of honour. If you fail to communicate effectively, it's **your** fault.

One area that can be troublesome is when your audience is mixed, with everyone having varying degrees of experience, understanding and knowledge. You don't want to bore the experts with your simplicity, nor dismiss the layperson with specialist terms and concepts. The solution can be as simple as setting out and explaining your specialist terms early in your delivery to try and bridge this gap. This is another balancing act – a paradoxical tightrope that needs to be walked. There will always be a time when you patronise or bore your experts, just as there will be times when you lose your laypeople. The trick is to try and minimise the number and impact of these events.

One approach to improve your effectiveness in communication is trying to adopt the terms and language of your audience. If you're talking to bankers – talk money. What works for a banker will probably not work well for a teacher or university professor. Use real-world examples whenever you can – especially when the examples are closely related to the activities and interests of your audience. This enhances attention spans and helps people to empathise with whatever you're trying to say. A local example is better than one from a distant place or country. Having your audience identify with the example makes it more powerful and effective.

LOCATION AND NATION

One area that requires additional attention relates to **where** your audience is from. Different places have different norms. They often have different languages. When dealing with different languages it becomes clear that, in the same manner that jargon use can restrict communication effectiveness, the use of vernacular and culture-specific idioms can do the same. Many people who learn a foreign language do so in a 'classical' style – without reference to the use of idioms and 'sayings'. The verbatim translation of many common idioms can be immensely confusing to the non-native speakers.

Idioms rarely survive direct translation. The German expression '*Ich habe hummeln in hintern*' translates as 'I have bumblebees in the bottom'. It takes a while to reach 'I have ants in my pants'. So many phrases are open to misinterpretation. If you are dealing with a multi-lingual audience, you have to identify the idioms, and find a suitable way to navigate through them. Many images and concepts that may make sense to, for example, Northern Europeans, will be obscure to Southeast Asian people. Idioms add colour and vibrancy to language, but you have to be aware of them, and provide a suitable replacement in the target language (if you are dealing with a mono-lingual audience) or provide a readily translatable alternative.

Just for reference, here are a few English idioms that don't cut the mustard (yes – that was deliberate):

- let the cat out of the bag;
- get the wrong end of the stick (a phrase that has a very nasty smelly origin);
- kick the bucket.

There are numerous examples of idioms from many countries and cultures. A TED blog[24] by Helene Batt and Kate Torgovnick May is very enlightening on the subject.

I have spent time assessing various training courses. One organisation I worked for was UK-based and provided exams and certifications for an almost exclusively UK student body. Many training organisations from around the world submitted their courses for assessment, hoping to become accredited and thereby opening up new

---

24 See https://blog.ted.com/40-idioms-that-cant-be-translated-literally/.

markets for their products. It became clear that some of the courses used terms and references that were specific to their countries of origin. Some US-based courses mentioned specific items of legislation that were only pertinent in the US. Others used US spelling or indicated prices in dollars. This is understandable to a degree, but a UK student body requires a different approach. We're all used to seeing American references in the UK, but training vendors offering a course for accreditation for a UK student body via a UK-based certifying assessment organisation should perhaps recognise these differing factors. Many of the courses failed initially to obtain accreditation and required editing. Some required so much fundamental change that they were withdrawn from the process. Such change was often difficult as some of the material was presented in video format, and some of the text was embedded in the videos themselves. Making the changes would not be easy, as the text was an image rather than digital characters.

Whatever medium you decide to use, remember that there will be circumstances that can invalidate your content, and it can be expensive and time-consuming to rectify such issues.

LEVEL AND ABSTRACTION

It's worth returning to a matter mentioned earlier. The 'level' you set for your communication is important and goes back to the 'paradox' referred to in the Introduction and Chapter 1.

- You have to communicate information in a manner that gives your audience what they need to carry out the thing (or things) you are asking them to do via your communication.
- There has to be enough information – but not too much.
- It has to be digestible in the timeframe available to your audience.
- It should cover all the necessary points without becoming burdensome to assimilate and to make a decision.
- A key part of working out your 'level' relates to your audience. You need to know who they are, where they are, what they do, and what they know (or don't know). Without knowing this and acting upon this knowledge, your efforts at communicating are less likely to succeed.

CONCLUSION

One size rarely fits all. Whilst it is normally impractical to provide a bespoke solution for every audience, perhaps the most practical approach to take is to meet the needs of the majority. This is a constant judgement call that has to be made, and to be able to do this requires you to listen, empathise and understand. This is an ongoing cyclical process that echoes many of the concepts that will be outlined later in this book. The need to measure your effectiveness, respond to feedback and react appropriately is key to success.

3   COMMUNICATION METHODS AND TOOLS

It's obvious that there are some questions you need to ask prior to setting up any sort of communication – be this an email or a structured comms programme. You can ask 'How?' What media or tools might you use? You can ask 'What?' What are the messages or learnings you want to pass on?[25]

So often people forget to ask 'Why?' This underpins everything. One approach is to be relatively formal and structured. In *Information Security and Employee Behaviour: How to Reduce Risk Through Employee Education, Training and Awareness*,[26] I set out a five-step approach. The steps are:

1. Manage by Fact;

2. Goals and Objectives;

3. Planning;

4. Implementation;

5. Feedback.

The model is simple and is very similar to others such as the 'Plan, Do, Study, Act' Deming Cycle[27] that is used in many ways for many purposes. There is further analysis on the Deming Cycle in Chapter 7. In the context of this chapter the key step is Number 2 – Goals and Objectives. **Why** are you communicating, and **what** are you trying to achieve? Much of the time you are probably looking to either pass on information or asking a question that requests information. Other times you may be seeking to influence someone to make a decision or take a particular action. All of these factors will influence what you communicate, how you do so, what media or channels you might use, when you do it, and to whom you do so.

This is a structured version of the old approach that involves writing your message – walking away for a few minutes before sending it, then checking it again prior to doing so. It may be worth seeking advice from someone else to check it out prior to dispatch. You want your communication to have the effect you want. Hastiness, negative emotions, lack

---

25 What, When, Why and How. What is what you are communicating, and what you need the audience to do and the impact to them. When is the timing of the comms. Why you are communicating, e.g. pilot group for enterprise change and what you want to gain, and then the How refers to the channels and tools to be used.

26 McIlwraith, A. (2006) *Information Security and Employee Behaviour: How to Reduce Risk Through Employee Education, Training and Awareness.* Aldershot, UK: Gower. 107.

27 The Deming Cycle Plan, Do, Study, Act (PDSA) concept forms part of a methodology used to introduce continual improvement into system and business development processes.

of focus and sloppiness can wreck what you want to achieve – and even set you back. I try very hard not to send messages when I'm angry – especially if I'm angry with the recipient. If writing an email, write your message, leave the 'To' field blank, and then wait for at least an hour. Read the message again, delete the rude words and have a think.

So – think before you send and be clear as to what it is you are trying to achieve.

Then you can decide on such things as:

- medium;
- tone;
- timing;
- who is on the 'CC' list (if you are using email of course. If not, think about who else might see the message besides the intended recipient);
- who is on the 'BCC' list (a potentially hairy area that needs thought).

You need to ask just **who** it is you're talking to. You need to know about their understanding of the issue, their level of expertise, their native language, their position in the organisation and how much time they have.

TOOLS

It would be easy to drift into a discussion on the merits and/or demerits of various tools and media. I think it prudent to limit discussions and become tool, medium and channel 'agnostic'. There are presentation tools like PowerPoint (and similar offerings such as Apple's Keynote) that serve a particular function and do it well. It's the users who make the mistakes – see the section 'How not to use PowerPoint' in the next chapter for a rant on the product.

There are obvious differences between various media – the undoubted versatility and effectiveness of the audio-visual medium is countered by the fact it is hard to edit once completed and takes up a load of memory and bandwidth if it's of any decent quality. I have discovered to my cost that one of the most difficult things to edit into a smooth deliverable is an audio-visual file with a voiceover. Editing sound, particularly voice, can be really difficult to do well. In many ways, the voiceover dictates the timings of the final offering. Sound editing is an art that gets really hairy.

There are a range of related issues that need attention, although not all will apply to every circumstance. There are rules and requirements of providing content that is accessible to all. In order to be compliant, this may require, for example, making text readable to people who are visually impaired. The same applies to text to voice readers – you may find you have to ensure your content can be delivered by these different routes. You may also need to consider the need to provide bi-lingual versions of your content. In England and Wales, government publications need both English and Welsh versions. This may be outside your control or capability, but the time and effort required to provide these variants needs to be factored in to any plans you have.

What **really** matters is the content, and the **way** in which it is delivered. You can have the highest definition HDMI video coupled with Dolby 5.1 audio, but it will be pointless if your content is poor. The best production values can be rendered meaningless quickly.

Very often, your choice of tool is a done deal. If the organisation you work for uses Microsoft products, it's likely you'll be limited to PowerPoint. If you need to store your files on a SharePoint[28] instance that is managed closely to avoid running out of disk space, you may have issues using hi-definition video or hosting Shareable Content Object Reference Model (SCORM)[29] compliant e-learning modules.

There are additional issues that will require attention in some organisations. One relates to corporate branding. You may be required to meet guidelines on colours, fonts and style. There are also many organisations (particularly in government) that require accessibility for all, with material being made suitable for screen-readers for both sight- and hearing-impaired audiences. As stated earlier, in the UK, many government publications (printed, online or otherwise) need to be published in both English and Welsh. The Scottish government has strong policies on the use of English, Gaelic, Scots, British Sign Language and some 150 minority languages. Factors such as these need to be taken into account.

The following sections set out aspects of communication that can relate to both the written and spoken word. They are meant to pass on ideas about how to structure and package your communications to make them more effective.

SCREEN-BASED TEXT AND PRECIS

What is clear is that the medium you use will influence the material you communicate. Written communication that's presented online as a web page generally has to be different from words presented on a printed page. Reading off a screen makes people impatient. Multiple sources suggest reading speeds for screen text are about one third slower compared to reading printed material. Many readers tend to 'skim' the text, seeking highlights and key points. If you don't grab attention within the first paragraph many readers will 'bail out'. There are some rules of thumb that can make screen-based text more effective – it's simply an exercise in precis.

The steps are:

- Write down what you want to say. Pause.
- Read it again and try and cut it by 50 per cent without losing any meaning.
- Arrange what's left into what you think is the right priority order. Pause.
- Read it again and try and cut it by 50 per cent without losing any meaning.

If you can do this and the remaining text feels readable and meaningful, you have created something that should work on a screen. It helps if you can place the more important elements in your text close to the beginning of your piece. Print journalists use a phrase, known as a 'hook', early in the piece to catch and retain attention. The 'hook' is often a summary or conclusion relating to the piece, with the following text supporting the

---

28 SharePoint is a Microsoft web-based collaborative platform that operates with Microsoft Office tools and data.

29 SCORM is a series of standards and specifications for web-based e-learning systems.

conclusion. Each of the following paragraphs should detail a single point or fact that supports the conclusion. This approach (known to some as the 'inverted pyramid') makes for snappy, compelling text that makes a point, catches attention and retains readership. One heuristic measurement (based on multiple sources) relates to human short-term memory, which retains information for between 10 and 30 seconds. Any communication message that exceeds these parameters cannot easily be absorbed and retained. If you can deliver a fact or message within this time, you can make your message easier to understand. You can double up and combine this with the 'Rule of Three' set out below. More information on short-term memory is provided in Chapter 5 in the section 'Detail – how much?'

THE RULE OF THREE

There is something magical about the number three. In his 1984 book *Our Masters' Voices: The Language and Body Language of Politics*, Maxwell J. Atkinson[30] provided a series of examples of how many public speakers use three-part phrases to telling effect. For example, Martin Luther King Jr used this 'tripling' concept in two phrases that worked together to provide emphasis and contrast in a speech called 'Non-violence and Racial Justice'. The phrases were:

- insult, injustice and exploitation;

which was followed a short time later in the speech;

- justice, good will and brotherhood.

The two phrases create a degree of tension (called by some 'binary opposition') that emphasise the point he was making.

The technique is not confined to political speeches. It is seen throughout literature and storytelling in many contexts. It's common in children's fairy tales (a sure sign that the approach uses a fundamental human communication channel). It's used extensively in advertising and public information communications. Neither is it restricted to short triads of words. Whole story structures use the Rule of Three. Ebenezer Scrooge is visited by three spirits in Dickens' *A Christmas Carol*. In just about every folk tale there's a similar theme. The Three Little Pigs were assailed by the Big Bad Wolf three times.

Further examples include:

- 'veni, vidi, vici' ('I came, I saw, I conquered' – attributed to Julius Caesar regarding the conquest of Britain);
- 'friends, Romans, countrymen' – Mark Antony's speech in Shakespeare's *Julius Caesar* (he gets everywhere that guy).

Many series of books are delivered as trilogies. It is the minimum number of entities that can create an acoustic rhythm. I've no idea why the Rule of Three works – but it does, especially if you can combine it with the eight second short-term memory heuristic mentioned above.

---

30 Atkinson, M.J. (1984) *Our Masters' Voices: The Language and Body Language of Politics*. London: Methuen.

EXAMPLES AND ANALOGIES

One useful tactic is to use examples of familiar objects, places and concepts to help your audience or readership to comprehend the size or disposition of anything. You can illustrate figures with something people can relate to. One commonly used illustration is 'the size of a football pitch'. Note that this works globally, as even the USA 'football'[31] pitches are of similar size to what everyone else in the world calls football. It can be used in multiples, for example 'the size of three football pitches'.

For some reason, Wales is used as an example measure of land area in the UK, as is the road distance from London to Edinburgh. I have a friend who continues to measure time in 'preps'. 'Prep' was the term used for a period in the evening when this person and his fellow boarding-school attendees were forced to do their homework (or 'prep' as it was known – this being a shortened term for 'preparation'). It was considered an inordinate length of time, and any event that lasted 'more than two preps' was indeed a marathon and was no doubt an endurance event. For the record, one 'prep' equals 90 minutes. If you are going to use examples, make them accessible and make sure your audience is going to understand them. Not everyone had to do prep.

Analogies can be very powerful. There is an initiative called The Analogies Project[32] that seeks to provide tales that reinforce learning. The section below is a piece I wrote for the project (published with permission) to illustrate how rules and practices in an organisation can become embedded – even when they are perhaps no longer applicable.

SEVEN UNWISE MONKEYS

So many security risks manifest because people behave in a manner that defies logic. If you are working in an organisation in which you find a behaviour or process that seems totally illogical, wasteful and stupid, there are normally three explanations. They are:

- there are issues or facts that you don't know about that have a bearing on the matter
- the organisation is indeed insane
- these behaviours or processes are an inherited legacy that have remained due to inertia

These legacy items often remain as part of company policy. The reasons for their existence are normally long gone. There is a delightful seven-step process I heard of recently regarding the development of company policy. It goes as follows:

---

31 If it were properly named, American football would be called 'hand egg'.

32 See https://theanalogiesproject.org/the-analogies/seven-unwise-monkeys-2.

1. Set up a cage and place five monkeys in it. Hang a banana on a string inside the cage and place a set of steps under it. After a while, a monkey will go to the steps and climb towards the banana. As soon as he touches the steps, spray all of the other monkeys with very cold water.

2. Soon after that, another monkey will attempt the steps. At this point, spray all the other monkeys with cold water. Pretty soon, when another tries to climb the stairs, the other monkeys will try to stop it by attacking it.

3. Remove one monkey from the cage and replace it with a new one. The new monkey will see the banana and try to climb the steps. All of the other monkeys will attack him.

4. After subsequent attempts and attacks, the monkey knows that if he tries to climb the steps, he will be attacked.

5. Next, remove another of the original five monkeys and replace it with a new one. The newcomer will go to the steps and be attacked. The previous newcomer will take part in the violence with enthusiasm, happy that it has been directed elsewhere.

6. Next, replace a third original monkey with a new one, then a fourth, then the fifth. Every time the newest monkey attempts the steps, he is attacked. Most of the monkeys that are beating him will have no idea why they were not permitted to climb the steps or why they are attacking the newest monkey.

7. After all the original monkeys have been replaced, none of the remaining monkeys have ever been sprayed with cold water. Nevertheless, no monkey ever again approaches the steps to try to reach the banana. Why? Because as far as they know that's the way it's always been done around here.

If you know all the facts, and are convinced the organisation is sane enough to plead, then you are left with the monkeys. Legacy and inertia manifest everywhere, and have a stealthy impact on the security of all organisations. The roof of the main railway station in New Delhi is designed to withstand the weight of three feet of snow. The gauge of most modern railways is based on the width of two harnessed horses. These are legacy issues.

When managing information risk, look for legacy. If you ever hear the phrase 'because that's the way we've always done it' you've found it. Eliminate it. There's nothing wrong with deep-seated, well-founded good practice, but few things are more potentially harmful than good intentions that have gone past their sell-by-date.

CONCLUSION

There is a phrase I've heard that I will repeat later on – a fool with a tool is still a fool. It's easy to become distracted by tools whilst forgetting that they are a means to an end. When I was young I was a very keen angler and bought many brightly coloured lures and other expensive gear that I presumed would make me a master fisherman. Other people seemed to get on better with a simple worm on a hook. You have to get the basics right – and then apply the tool!

4   STORYTELLING

UBIQUITY, CYCLES AND HARDWIRED FOR CHILDREN

The purpose of this chapter is to set out how telling stories is one of the most powerful ways in which information can be passed on, and that people learn more from hearing this information in a story-based context. It is also an immensely powerful medium for persuading people to perform specific actions and develop changed attitudes. There are other similar human behaviour elements that are ubiquitous and exist in almost every culture. One is music. Different cultures may use different musical scales. The classical European scale feels and sounds very different from the Indian, Chinese and Arabic scales, but there are significant links between them as well. Without delving too deeply into the complexities of musical theory, the core elements of the major pentatonic scale (also referred to as the Pythagorean scale) is present in every major musical culture across the globe. Anyone who plays blues guitar understands pentatonic notes. Another human behaviour element is also ubiquitous – storytelling. Kendall Haven, author of *Story Proof*[33] and *Story Smart*[34] affirms the following:

> Your brain has been evolutionarily hardwired to think, to understand, to make sense, and to remember in specific story terms and elements.[35]

These story terms and elements have been tested across cultures, and it is clear that people respond to stories that use a particular structure that looks something like this:

- The situation is 'normal' – the status quo is stable.

- Someone (aka 'the character') has an idea – which transmutes into a goal – and wants to achieve it. This is allied to a clear, credible motive.

- The character cannot reach the goal because they are prevented from doing so by barriers and obstacles – which introduce jeopardy through the potential for failure and negative consequences (such as *inter alia* loss of status or even death).

- A struggle ensues – and additional characters and related assistance is uncovered that provides a means to meet the goal.

---

33 Haven, K. (2007) *Story Proof* (1st ed.). London: Bloomsbury Publishing.

34 Haven, K. (2014) *Story Smart: Using the Science of Story to Persuade, Influence, Inspire, and Teach.* London: Bloomsbury Academic.

35 See https://www.kendallhaven.com/.

- Once the goal is reached a new status quo is set up. This remains in place until the new story kicks in. There is a twist in this cycle – a story that features a failure to achieve the goal is called 'a tragedy'.

If you have any doubts about the efficacy and ubiquity of this structure, check out the following examples:

- The *Epic of Gilgamesh* – an epic poem from ancient Mesopotamia – regarded as one of the earliest examples of religious literature – written c. 2100–1200 BCE.
- The *Bhagavad Gita* ('Song of God' or 'Song of the Lord') – one of the most important religious texts of Hinduism – written c. 50 BCE.
- The *Tale of Genji* – a classic work of Japanese literature – written c. 1000 CE.
- *Beowulf* – an Old English epic poem in the tradition of Germanic heroic legend – written c. 975–1025 CE.
- The Harry Potter series.
- The Lord of the Rings trilogy.

The cycle can be summarised this:

old status > clear goal > obstacles > external assistance > struggle > new status

The reason stories work is that humans are hardwired to understand them, and deviation from the structure results in unsatisfactory stories, and a poorer communications experience. There's a reason why all cultures have morality tales and warning tales for children. They work.

HOW CAN WE USE STORIES IN THE WORKPLACE?

How not to use PowerPoint

When I first started serious work (that being IT security stuff), I attended many professional conferences. One was called COMPSEC (Computer Security I guess). It was held annually at the QEII Centre in Westminster, London. I even presented there at least once. It was the acme of professional gatherings as far as I was concerned at the time. I chose the sessions I was interested in. I armed myself with conference notepaper and a sharp pencil. I sat and had every intention to listen, concentrate and learn. If my mind wandered, I castigated myself for my lack of professionalism, focus and drive. However – my mind did wander. I tried to focus, and in some cases, it worked. I learned things. I absorbed facts and insight. Most of the time, this did not happen. I can honestly say that about 75 per cent of the sessions I sat through were a waste of time. The material might have been suitable for a paper or even an email. Having scores of people sat down, bored to tears by your droning is not a good look, not a good listen, and not a good use of time, energy or emotional resources.

How do you break this negativity? Get people to tell stories.

A scheme I've developed has helped me assemble slide decks and accompanying presentations and has served me pretty well. I did this without knowing about the 'old status > clear goal > obstacles > external assistance > struggle > new status' cycle. I wrote what I called, perhaps a little pretentiously, 'librettos' – outlines of the words I wanted to use to when presenting. They were not scripts because as soon as you have a verbatim script when presenting live someone will interject with a comment or question and cripple your flow. You have to be adaptable. The libretto was verbal in origin. I wrote down the words I said in my head as if I were telling a public story. The slides accompanied the words – they were used for what I called 'visual punctuation'. I now try to assemble slide decks that have no words – just pictures. This is because PowerPoint is a visual tool. You might have a slide title – even a series of bullet points – but the main idea as far as I can tell is to present images to accompany a presentation – which is verbal. A PowerPoint presentation is an audio-visual offering. A PowerPoint deck is **not** a document.

This approach has not always met with universal approval. I have been chastised by reviewers (who want to see my slides before the conference, seminar or gathering) because 'there are no words'. I have often responded with 'correct – I'm delivering a presentation, not a document'. I often send reviewers my libretto in the form of 'speaker notes' in PowerPoint. To my continual surprise, I often have people reviewing the words and providing tracked 'corrections' as if they were part of a formal paper rather than the words acting as support for a verbal presentation. I nearly always ignore these insertions unless they are such things as specific factual corrections or proper explanations of terms. I have even had people demand I insert a detailed numeric table into one of my slide decks for no purpose other than to show that we had some numbers behind our thinking. If you have details such as tables or a serious amount of text (such as a formal report) – deliver it as an accompanying PDF or paper document.

> Don't try and document your material on a slide. It's not what it's for. If you think it is – you are wrong.

HOW TO TELL A STORY

What is important to remember is that you should have a purpose behind your story.

You're telling it for a reason – normally to convince people to act or think in a particular way. In 1998, Robert McKee published *Story: Substance, Structure, Style, and the Principles of Screenwriting*.[36] In it he asserts that stories

> fulfil a profound human need to grasp the patterns of living—not merely as an intellectual exercise, but within a very personal, emotional experience.

You have to persuade people at an emotional level. There is more information on this emotional element to communication in Chapter 1 in the section 'To persuade', and in Chapter 11. It may also be helpful to look at the situation, task, action and result (STAR) method set out in Chapter 7 of this book.

---

36 McKee, R. (1998) *Story: Substance, Structure, Style and the Principles of Screenwriting.* London: Methuen.

The traditional way in which most leaders seek to persuade others to act is by using what McKee calls 'conventional rhetoric'. This approach requires you (as the communicator) to set out the goal, and then set out what we need to do to meet it. The process normally includes some accompanying facts, figures and quotations from recognised authorities. This can work, but it operates at an intellectual and logical level – not the emotional level. This is important because you will almost inevitably be fighting your listeners. This is because each of them has their own facts, figures and authoritative quotations at the ready – and they will argue with you internally. Remember that you need to present an emotional case as well as a logical case if you want to persuade people to your point of view.

Therefore, the more powerful means to break through this resistance is to engage with your listeners at an emotional level. Remember the 'old status > clear goal > obstacles > external assistance > struggle > new status' cycle. McKee uses a screen-writer term that describes the 'obstacle' element – he calls it the 'inciting event'. This is the thing that messes up the 'character'. The story needs to relate how the character deals with uncertainty, lack of cooperation, lack of resources, risks, jeopardy – and then goes about dealing with them and restoring balance. You only have to look at the stories behind the Star Wars films to see this approach achieved with mastery. Even the scripts talk openly about 'restoring balance'. McKee suggests that the core element is the 'fundamental conflict between subjective expectation and cruel reality'.[37]

The following steps are provided for guidance.

- Begin by setting out your goal. What are you trying to get your audience to think or do? We've already affirmed that stories work well by setting out some ethic or moral. This is the essence of your story. If you can distil your moral into a straightforward and memorable phrase all the better.

- Find an example from which to build your story. It can be from personal experiences or those of someone you know. It helps if the listeners are familiar with the story's subject or environment. There is nothing as effective as a personal or local example. There is also nothing more effective than a tale that involves recovery from failure or a setback. Remember that the purpose is not to present the storyteller in a heroic light. This will alienate a section of the audience and distract from the core message. You need to engage with them and make them find empathy and identify with the protagonists. The audience or readership are not there to give you a boost.

- The 'obstacle' and 'struggle' elements are the things that give your story colour and life. Without them the story will be nothing more than a chronological list of events. People like a bit of pain and anxiety, as well as a dose of jeopardy. They like to feel included in the team that's going to deal with it.

There are a couple of obvious truths that need to be adhered too. Firstly, try and keep your story in line with the experience and understanding of your listeners. This works in the same way as using real-world examples when providing training. The closer to your listeners' experience you can weave your tale, the more resonance you can achieve.

---

37 Ibid.

Also remember not to clutter up your tale with unnecessary detail. It's distracting and can crowd out your core moral or message. You'll need some detail, but this is to set the scene and the ambience.

When you hear a famed raconteur delivering their story in the pub, you often find that the delivery has been honed and refined. In short, a good storyteller has normally had the advantage of practice. Do the same. Sometimes you will make a mistake but learn from this and hone your delivery. This approach has to be set against the possibility of repeating your tale to the same people. Repetition can reduce the impact, so be aware of who is listening.

A friend and former colleague worked with me as a very capable information security architect. He was an extrovert and could hold an audience with stories and tales and was great company and very funny. It came only as a slight surprise when he told me he had undergone a training course on how to be a stand-up comedian. He now makes a living as a part-time architect and a part-time stand-up. He did tell me that the lessons he learned on how to construct a comedy set were the most useful he had ever taken as regards creating a presentation.

A joke is a story with a particular framework – often using the Rule of Three outlined above (a Scouser, a Brummie and a Cockney walked into a pub – there's that magic number three again). The other thing he mentioned was that he became more effective (essentially funnier) the more he practiced.

A raconteur is doing the right thing – honing their delivery. You can do the same with your presentations and stories.

The best work proposal I ever worked on was for a large-scale, multi-year UK government contract. I was on the 'bid team', and we all formed a jolly band of comrades who worked very hard to develop a compelling written proposal. It worked. We got through to the final round which involved a full team presentation to the most senior persons in the relevant government department – and more besides, as they hauled in senior seniors from their parent government department, as well as representatives from the relevant minister. The person who led the team did something I've never seen done before. He made us practice our presentations many, many times. He brought in an external coach who critiqued our slides and verbal delivery to death. Our presentations were videoed, and we all had to watch ourselves as people commented on our style, delivery, dress-sense and body language. It was excruciating at times. I recall I presented my piece at least 15 times – probably more. We turned up at the client, did our piece, cracked our now well-honed jokes, and generally smashed it. Such bids and proposals are awarded marks as part of the selection process, and these are used to guide the final decision. We scored 100 per cent for our presentation – something I've never seen before or since. As the great golfer Gary Player is reputed to have said – 'you know, the more I practice the luckier I get'.

If you practice, you make your own luck.

The power of the story structure is immense. It's hardwired into people, and they are programmed to receive, process and remember stories. A story is easier to remember than a flowchart, a series of bullet points or even a graph. Note that good images are very powerful when supplementing a story, so plan your slide deck accordingly.

NON-VERBAL COMMUNICATION

One of the key aspects of collaboration is empathy.

This is a fundamental human skill that if undertaken positively will enhance any attempt at communication and collaboration. Establishing empathy requires more than words and well-presented graphics. With the advent of remote working becoming commonplace, there's one thing that you may think is less important than previously – non-verbal communication. Tools such as MS Teams and Zoom saved many organisations during the COVID-19 pandemic. What many people missed was what some termed 'side-band' communication – the non-verbal cues that express emotion and convey subtle meaning. This goes beyond facial expressions – it involves the entire body. Given that Zoom calls tend to show heads only, there's no doubt it's less effective than face-to-face meetings.

There is a whole area of study linked to non-verbal communication, and include subjects that end with the letters 'ics' – such as:

- chronemics;
- haptics;
- kinesics;
- olfactics;
- proxemics;
- vocalics.

Chronemics relates to time, haptics to touch. Kinesics relates to body movements and facial expressions. Olfactics concerns itself with smell, proxemics with space (personal space and so forth), and vocalics deals with tone of voice and similar – perhaps an intruder in a list of non-verbal subjects. It's pretty obvious that Zoom calls cannot utilise smell, touch or personal space. What is clear is that collaborative behaviour is supported by making best use of some of these elements. What is also clear is that non-verbal communication conveys a significant percentage of the total – with some authorities suggesting this is as much as over 60 per cent.[38]

This whole area is not disconnected from the material presented in this chapter. It's also connected to the concept of active listening discussed in Chapter 7. The ideas are all mutually connected and reinforce the benefits from each other. Your body language should convey the fact that you **are** actually listening to someone. Even on a Zoom call,

---

[38] Burgoon, J.K., Guerrero, L.K. and Floyd, K (2011) *Nonverbal Communication*. Boston, MA: Allyn & Bacon.

the equivalent of eye-contact is important. Look at the camera – don't look down at your phone. One hint is to make sure your camera is located close to your screen. A side-mounted camera shows you staring away from the conversation whilst looking at your screen.

You can react to what's being said by nodding in agreement and reacting facially in an appropriate manner. It is possible to use hand gestures on camera – palms up to indicate openness and agreement. However, there's need for caution. There is a strong cultural aspect in non-verbal communication. What can be considered a simple two-fingered gesture to indicate the number two can be readily interpreted in some countries as an aggressive insult. An open palm with fingers raised pushed towards another is considered deeply insulting in others. A nod of the head can indicate 'yes', with a shake of the head indicating 'no'. In some cultures, the exact opposite is true.

What is important to understand is that meaning is enhanced non-verbally with all senses engaged. Having established that non-verbal communication could convey over 60 per cent of your total message, it is received by the senses in varying degrees – typically 83 per cent sight, 11 per cent hearing, 3 per cent smell, 2 per cent touch and 1 per cent taste.[39] Perhaps this reduces the need to convey smell during a Zoom call. It certainly reinforces the need to be **seen** to engage, because without this your ability to collaborate is immediately reduced. It is very important as a means to establish empathy.

You need to listen and be seen to listen. You need to engage at an emotional level. If you don't, people will spot it, because we are all very good at reading non-verbal signs. We can easily spot even the slightest raised eyebrow that indicates disagreement. We know when someone's zoning out on a call – even in Zoom. It's also obvious when you're browsing. In short, look up and engage using facial expressions, posture and hand gestures. This becomes especially true when face-to-face and when telling a story.

As with all aspects of communication, be aware of your audience, and try to ensure you avoid counter-cultural gestures and actions – especially if they may be considered offensive. It's sometimes worth doing some research into any cultures you may not be familiar with. You might avoid some of the obvious errors.

THE LONGEVITY AND POWER OF STORIES

If you think that the concept of stories is a bit feeble and lacks the empiricism and factual integrity of more formal means of communication, I ask that you consider the following.

When I was young my father told me a story he had been told by a very elderly relative. It outlined a stormy night on the Scottish Hebridean island of North Uist and involved a small patch of land known as Baleshare (Scottish Gaelic: *Baile Sear*) that is now a low-lying island that lies to the south-west of North Uist that can be accessed by a causeway.

---

39 Pease, B. and Pease, A. (2004) *The Definitive Book of Body Language.* New York: Bantam Books.

According to the story it had previously been attached to the main island. The story spoke very specifically of the strength and direction of the storm winds, the state of the tide and the scenes of havoc as the sea invaded the land and cut Baleshare off. The story spoke of several distinct events including the destruction of a land bridge to the township of Kirkibost, 100 metres to the north, and the loss of a nearby village. Note that Baleshare means 'east farm' or 'east town' in Gaelic. There was possibly a related 'west town', perhaps destroyed in the storm.

I later read (in my then capacity as a student studying geography at Aberdeen University) a geomorphological study of Baleshare that described the exact same events in the exact same order – detailing the storm winds, the tide and the loss of land. The study confirmed the verbal story's details and chronology. What did surprise me was that the story covered events that occurred in the 16th century – being passed down verbally through multiple generations whilst preserving factual integrity for more than 400 years.

You don't get that in an Excel table that's been cut and pasted into a PowerPoint deck, or a flowchart, a series of bullet points or even a graph. You can only get it in a story.

CONCLUSION

Stories are universal. They are hard-wired into the way we, as humans, learn and understand things. Raw facts are less use if they are given with no context. Examples of usage and verbal illustrations of pitfalls provide the best means of teaching people. Telling stories is a skill that can be learned, and there's no doubt that practice will improve your delivery, as does preparing yourself in such a way that you can anticipate possible questions and respond using prepared answers. These 'prepared answers' might well be considered part of your 'back-story'. They are part of the context of the information you're trying to impart. Stories are not 'nice-to-haves' to support your cause. They are at it's heart and should be treated as such.

5   PRESENTING DATA AND INFORMATION

DATA AND INFORMATION – WHAT'S THE DIFFERENCE?

There is often some confusion about the words 'data' and 'information'. Data tends to be individual items – facts and numbers. The best analogy I know is as follows:

The following list of items is data:

- 225g softened butter;
- 225g golden caster sugar;
- 4 large eggs;
- ½ lemon, zested;
- 1 tsp vanilla extract;
- 225g self-raising flour;
- splash of milk;
- optional fillings of lemon curd, jam, lightly whipped cream;
- icing sugar for dusting.

The data can be visualised as all the above ingredients set out on a table. They are of limited use to anyone in their native, raw state. They need to be processed and converted into something else. A sponge cake is information. The recipe is the process by which the data is converted into information. Information has structure and meaning that can only be ascertained once an appropriate process has been applied to data.

If you want to tell someone something with the intention of, for example, changing their minds about something, you probably need to provide information – not data. Give them a cake.

DETAIL – HOW MUCH?

I recall a client who required a monthly report on their status regarding the multiple operational risks they faced. This was part of the standard governance structure they used to track risks, manning levels, expenditure and so forth.

The report was delivered at a fairly intensive four-hour meeting that had many attendees representing the many interested parties – both internal and external to the organisation. The risks they faced were significant – including theft of intellectual property, fraud, fire, flood and activism. The report was created by several teams. The IT security team had an individual who was earnest, keen and very technically capable. His report took a long time to deliver. It included multiple slides of immense detail – that were unreadable even when displayed on the very large screen provided for the meeting. He insisted, amongst other things, on reporting **all** the changes that had been made in the preceding month on **all** the various switches and routers in what was an extensive international network. Basically, he delivered a stream of data in table format to a very senior audience who did not truly understand the data nor its context. In summary – he failed.

There is another question that needs answering – how much data/information should you present? I mentioned above the technical expert delivering crowded presentation screens that contain large amounts of data. The fact is – there is a limit to what people can absorb and retain. Long detailed lists are all very well if they are written down and used for reference. They are less useful when delivered verbally.

There are some rules of thumb that can help to shape your communication, especially if you are delivering verbally with support from a presentation slide deck. If you have a bulleted list of three bullets it can be remembered – especially if the bullets are short (refer to Chapter 3 on the Rule of Three). Just about every public information campaign uses this technique. The recently revived 1970s road safety campaign slogan 'Think once, think twice, think bike' resonates down the years. Nike's 'Just do it' slogan and 'Stay Home. Save Lives. Protect the NHS' used by the UK government during the 2020–2021 COVID-19 pandemic will be long remembered.

Another rule of thumb relates to short-term memory. We are all able to retain and recall a number of pieces of information for a short time.

In 1956 research by cognitive psychologist George A. Miller of Harvard University's Department of Psychology was published in an edition of *Psychological Review* in a paper titled 'The magical number seven, plus or minus two'.[40] The article is cited frequently and suggests that the number of objects an average human can hold in short-term memory is about seven (plus or minus two). There are a number of other factors that affect this, such as the volume of information in each object, but the core assertion remains valid. I have already mentioned presentation slides that are crowded with data – using multiple bullets (objects perhaps?) and flooding the viewer. If you are preparing presentation slides, one of the key things to remember is that if you want your audience to remember things and have the ability to follow a cogent train of thought, do not exceed seven bullet points. Better still, be pragmatic and stick to five. You also need to remember that short-term memory is just that – short term. It will degrade with time, additional input and distraction. You have to be able to use the short-term recall to establish a single assertion. It is the **result** of the five bullets that will ultimately

40 Miller, G. (1956) The magical number seven, plus or minus two: some limits on our capacity for processing information. *Psychological Review*, 63 (2). 81–97.

be remembered. If you have too many bullets, very little will be retained, and the core message will be diluted. You may well fail.

Interpretation of data and information is also critical. There are many examples of people making assertions based on data. This can be compelling, especially if one can visualise the data through means such as graphs and diagrams (more on this later).

It's important to have the right data because it is from this that you can interpret it into a form that can be used to make decisions. Presenting router and switch configurations to board-level executives who have limited time, limited bandwidth and limited detailed understanding will do you no good whatsoever. It will probably cause you harm, damage your reputation and risk you losing the chance to communicate what really matters to some important people. Refer to Chapter 2 – 'Know your audience' for more information on this matter.

The above sections do not mean I'm disrespecting data and bigging up information. Data is fundamental and needs to be current, complete, correct and in a usable format. It must have integrity. Suitable data meets all these tests. If you are reporting on events that happened in July, the data should include all the data relating to events in July. This sounds obvious, but without this completeness, you will be left guessing. You also need to trust the source of the data. Before you can begin processing and interpreting information, you need to be sure of your source.

TRUSTED SOURCES

When I was young, I remember having arguments in school wherein my opponents would often counter any challenge regarding the truth of their statements with the retort 'I read it in a book.' If it's in a book, it must be true ran the logic. The current equivalent is 'I did my research – it's on the internet.'

A reliable source of data is essential. This before you get into the murky world of data interpretation – something we'll deal with in a minute.

I would trust the statistics provided by the UK government Office for National Statistics (ONS) or the United States Census Bureau (USCB) more readily than statistics provided without verified sources by any political party. When dealing with any kind of formal research data – particularly scientific research data – it needs to be credible. To be scientifically credible, the work must be:

- published in a reputable journal;
- peer reviewed;
- assessed along (as a minimum) the following three dimensions:
  - transparency of method and data;
  - be reproduceable and robust;
  - replicable.

It's arguable as to what 'reputable' means as this is open to all sorts of debate. It could be that being reputable means that the journal has become part of the establishment and is therefore biased and therefore **not** credible. The same issue pertains to the term 'peer' – are scientists operating in a cabal to fetter free thinkers? For the sake of this piece, I'll respond to the question with 'No.'

The true beauty of the scientific method is that if credible evidence emerges that disproves an earlier established world view, the previous mindset is erased. Evidence trumps all. Facts stand for themselves, and good data resists challenge. Bad data does not.

DATA AND INFORMATION VISUALISATION

There is a quotation (with a number of variants) attributed to a triumvirate of physicists – Albert Einstein, Ernest Rutherford and Richard Feynman – that states:

> If you can't explain it simply you don't understand it well enough.

Whatever the truth regarding the quotation, explaining complex things to non-specialists is challenging. You can use carefully chosen words and subtle levels of abstraction. You can use Miller's law on the effectiveness of the number seven outlined above. You can use analogies. All of these are powerful and are certainly not mutually exclusive. However, there's one approach that knocks all of these into a cocked hat. It is a drawing. If you can draw what it is you're trying to say, you are well on the way to improving your communication. Leonardo da Vinci is cited as stating that a poet would be 'overcome by sleep and hunger before describing with words what a painter is able to convey in an instant'. Napoleon Bonaparte is credited with saying *'Un bon croquis vaut mieux qu'un long discours'* – 'a good sketch is better than a long speech'.

Before we all go off to oil painting classes and planning continental military campaigns, it's worth looking at what we can do to present complexity in clear and accessible graphic formats.

As a species, we use visual cues to a huge extent. 'Data visualisation' provides an effective, rapid means to communicate information using visual information, that is, pictures, and can avoid the complexity of words.

The first tool of this type I saw was being used by Sussex Police to support criminal investigations. The tool provided visualisation and analysis of huge amounts of data from multiple disparate data sources to aid criminal investigation. It was possible to look at a graphic assembled from thousands of data points and connections between them, and from these pictures discover hitherto hidden connections. The example I saw connected data about bank accounts, lawyers, estate agents and accountants, and revealed an extensive and cunning web of fraudulent property transactions. The data in its raw form was (to a human) meaningless. Once shown as multiple connections in a picture it became easy for me to see patterns. This is something people are pretty good at.

When combined with the evolving techniques that are emerging relating to Big Data, data visualisation can become an essential communication tool. It can now go beyond standard representations such as pie charts and line graphs, and utilise images based on trend analyses, word clouds and geographic maps.

Such visualisation is not new. In 1854, an English medical doctor called John Snow was working on treating a significant cholera epidemic in London. At the time the established theory was that cholera (and most other diseases) was airborne (note that the word 'malaria' means 'bad air' in Latin – an example of this established theory from the distant past). He established that the source of the outbreak was a public water pump and managed to persuade authorities to remove the handle. It worked, and the outbreak fizzled out. One of the main supporting elements in this work was a simple street map that set out where the disease occurred. It was one of the first such uses of a map, and it remains very striking.

Figure 5.1 Dr John Snow's cholera map (Source: John Snow, 1854 originally published by C.F. Cheffins, Lith, Southampton Buildings, London)

The dot in the centre of the map in Broad Street shows the pump in question. It's pretty obvious where the source of the disease is likely to be, and this helped Dr Snow overcome the inertia of 'established theory'. Dr Snow realised that people in power needed to understand that treating the outbreak required them to see the whole picture rather than looking at individual cases of disease. His map was key to providing that understanding.

Visualisation allows you to:

- See the big picture.
- Identify significance.

- Make informed decisions.
- Track trends over time.

The rules that apply to using data, information, themes and ideas that are known to your audience apply to pictures as much as to words (whether written or spoken). The picture has to be relevant to the audience – using concepts they are familiar with.

- charts (including bubble charts, dot distribution maps);
- tables;
- graphs (including bullet graphs, histograms, scatter plots);
- maps;
- dashboards (including timelines, heat maps);
- word clouds.

CONCLUSION

You may recall my likening a list of ingredients to data and a cake to information. The way you present information is very similar to the way you need to provide overviews and precis of written text. No one is disputing the fundamental importance of data – remember that the devil is indeed in the detail. In the same way you have to deliver your words in an audience-appropriate manner, you have to do the same with data and information. Horses for courses for every occasion.

6   INTERPRETATION OF DATA

The text below (published with permission) is an extract from another piece I wrote for the Analogies Project.[41] It concerns how people can perceive information and experience, and come to the wrong conclusion:

> Complex systems don't behave in simple ways. You can't flick a switch and see an immediate, predictable, mechanical response. So often you hear someone complaining about a cold spell during the summer, and make a fatuously idiotic statement such as 'well, what's all this global warming about then? Why is it cold and rainy?' The answer is simple; the fatuous idiot is failing to understand the difference between climate and weather.
>
> - Weather is tactical.
> - Climate is strategic.
>
> ...
>
> You could look at many long term trends, and then select a section of it that runs counter to the overall trend. This seems to contradict the long term. So it goes for climate change. If all you remember is a couple of cold summers, then you may well denigrate the current climate change theories. Given the mass of evidence, you would be wrong.

Selective choices of data and information for interpretation to ensure the 'right answer' emerges does no service to anyone. It will be found out, although so often it's the case that the damage is done before a correction is made. If you are operating on a selective set of data, be up front about it. There may be good reasons for doing so – but remember that transparency is one of the three dimensions required of quality, peer-reviewed data.

To determine how any information or data is interpreted and perceived, you have to look firstly at the 'lens' through which it is viewed. We are all subject to a distortion of perception known as 'confirmation bias'.

When listening or reading, we all have a tendency to unconsciously select information that supports our point of view. We also tend to dismiss information that runs counter to our view. We also have an ingrained habit of, when presented with information that is ambiguous, unconsciously interpreting the information in a way that agrees with our

---

41 See https://theanalogiesproject.org/.

own views. This habit becomes more evident when views are strongly held, when the subject matter engenders significant emotion, or when a particular course of events or circumstances is deemed highly desirable. This tendency is called confirmation bias.

CONFIRMATION BIAS

The effects of confirmation bias can be extreme. They can be counter-intuitive. For example, two people may hold different views, but when presented with the same evidence, they can actually become more polarised in their disagreements. In many cases, a point of view may persist even when someone is presented with sound evidence that contradicts it. This is often exacerbated when two unsound points of view are combined to make a totally false assumption – people have an inbuilt tendency to seek simplistic 'cause and effect' relationships between events. This is why the climate change example set out above is so pertinent. It seems we are hardwired to seek simple 'cause and effect' situations. It's probably an innate survival mechanism at work.

This paragraph is important. If we are to learn how to interpret data and information, we must learn to be aware of **our own** innate tendencies. We must 'unlearn' inbuilt behaviours and learn to use different lenses when trying to be objective and clear-minded. It isn't easy. The brightest and biggest minds are as afflicted as the rest of us (not that I'm suggesting any readers are dumb or have tiny minds).

COMMUNICATION INTENTION

One simple tool you can use is through trying to understand the intention of the communication that provides the information. This is the beginning of working out what lens to use. It has undertones of such human elements as empathy and true listening. When being empathetic, you have to put yourself into another's shoes. You need to understand what lens the author is using when creating their speech, paper or presentation. What do they want us to do or think? Are they seeking to educate, inform or persuade us?

Sometimes it is completely obvious why someone is talking to us. They often state, up front, what it is they are doing. It certainly behoves anyone who is delivering information to declare upfront what their intention is. Unfortunately, this does not always happen. Indeed, it is sometimes the case that a communicator deliberately hides their intention. This is most common in cases when someone is seeking to persuade us to perform an action or form an opinion. This approach normally falls into the arena of advertisers and politicians – but not exclusively so.

Persuasion attempts can be detected. Robert Beno Cialdini, the Regents' Professor Emeritus of Psychology and Marketing at Arizona State University, created six 'Principles of Influence'[42] that defined how people can be influenced or persuaded. These are reciprocity, commitment and consistency, consensus or social proof, authority, liking and scarcity.

---

42 Cialdini, R. (1984) *Influence: The Psychology of Persuasion.* New York: Morrow.

Few attempts at persuasion involve all six principles, but it's worth knowing that they are often used in certain combinations.

The concept of **reciprocity** is based on the premise that people, by nature, feel obliged to provide something in return to those if they've been given something previously. Why do you think vendors provide giveaway 'swag' at trade fairs and conferences?

Commitment is based on the premise that people have an innate need to be consistent. This is related to the mindset that makes us resist changing our minds even when presented with new, contradictory, data.

Social proof (or consensus) relates to how people revert to doing things in the same way as others around them do. Anyone seeking to press your 'conform' button is quite likely to be trying to persuade you – perhaps covertly.

If you've ever wondered why adverts are full of white-coated doctors and dentists (or some other **authority** figure) it's because we do have a habit of doing as asked if the request or order comes from such a person.

The best example of this is an experiment performed in the 1960s by Stanley Milgram, a psychologist based at Yale University. He performed a famous experiment wherein the experiment's subjects were convinced to apply what they thought were powerful electric shocks to other people they did not know. They were persuaded by a white-coated authoritative figure who, if the subject became unwilling to administer further 'shocks' would be told that 'The experiment requires that you continue.'[43] Nearly 60 per cent of subjects were willing to deliver what they thought were dangerous shocks. Previous estimates suggested that the number should have been around 4 per cent. The power of perceived authority is massive. It's important to remember that the shocks were not real, and that the 'victims' were actors, as were the white-coated authority figures. Using authority figures in any communication is a clue that someone is trying to use your natural tendency to trust authority figures to their advantage.

It's fairly obvious that it's more likely you'll respond well to someone you like than to someone you don't. **Liking** can be based on relatively shallow things like physical attractiveness. A communication seeking to persuade you may well seek to establish such things as shared interests. This has implications regarding how you react to received information. Sometimes you have to be aware that you have unconscious bias towards certain people and will make unconscious allowances for them. Stripping out emotion can help you see things more clearly.

The final principle is used by advertisers and fraudster alike – I know it's hard to tell the difference at times. **Scarcity** is used to give the impression that the thing you want is either scarce, in limited supply, or that the supply is tightly time-bounded. If anyone uses the approach of 'one-time offer' or 'today only' it is doubtless because they are

---

43 Milgram, S. (1963) Behavioral study of obedience. *The Journal of Abnormal and Social Psychology*, 67 (4). 371–378.

trying to persuade you. The 'fear of missing out' is a real thing, and we are all subject to it. The trick is to spot it and not respond. This is why my bank's internet app provides advice on what to do when setting up a new payee around this aspect of our psychology.

Whatever the intention of the communication, there is a particular characteristic that need to be understood. The concepts of formal and informal communication relate to two things – the status of the communications, and the style of the language used.

COMMUNICATION STATUS

In terms of status, a formal communication tends to carry some degree of authority. It normally follows a set, agreed procedure, and relates to the formal delivery of information. It often tends to require a mandatory response. Examples include notice of:

- HR proceedings against an employee;
- a pay rise;
- a change in terms and conditions;
- the introduction of new rules.

There is a tendency to occasionally use language that is deemed 'formal' but is in fact unclear. An article I read in *The Guardian* concerning social care contained a paragraph that has stuck with me:

Why, for example, do inspectors (whose reports are all public documents) come up with 'localised lighting to beds' for bedside lamps? Or 'hot water outlets' for taps. Or 'nutritional management' for food? And they must surely know that phrases such as continuity of care, inter-agency and multi-disciplinary, domiciliary care and self-advocacy are meaningless to the outside world. So why use them?[44]

When you see this type of content, it's often because the writer is seeking to appear professional and solid. The reality is that they reduce their effectiveness. He also wrote:

If something can be read and understood at the first time of asking, then it's good writing. Simple as that. No matter that it's grammatically correct, well structured and displaying a wide vocabulary: if it's not understood, it's poor writing.

You have to see through the strangled language and tone to make sure that you understand whether the communication is formal or informal. This may well dictate how you respond, and often, how quickly you respond.

Responding to any communication normally needs you to use the same style and approximate format of the original. A formal letter normally needs a formal letter in response. It need not be the only format you use to respond. A letter backed up by a timely phone call can increase its effectiveness. Needless to say, it's normally sensible

---

44 Hopkins, G. (2000) *Why bureaucratic jargon is just a pompous waste of words*. The Guardian, Guardian News and Media. Available from https://www.theguardian.com/society/2000/sep/13/guardiansocietysupplement13.

(and most probably, polite) to respond to any questions or requests for information – even if it's just a note acknowledging the question or request (this is important if you are trying **not** to answer immediately).

The tone of voice (a concept that can apply to the written word as readily as the spoken word) should normally reflect that of the original. Responding to a letter signed by 'Sir Antony Miles KC' with the opening 'Hi Tony' may not elicit a positive reaction. Informality has its place, as do such conventions as 'text speak' (OMG – did I jst sy tht 2 u?) but you must consider the recipient. I am very old now and refuse to indulge in text speak and avoid emojis – although I do present random ones sometimes either in the hope that I appear 'hip', or to confuse young people, which is not difficult.

The response needs to be clear and readable. Remember Graham Hopkins' note above stating 'if it's not understood, it's poor writing'. You have to assess what you have received before responding. Whilst there are no set rules, it's worth using a checklist. I make no claim that this is complete:

- Is the communication formal or informal? (respond appropriately)
- What is being asked of me? (write a short list of actions required to make sure you pick up all the points)
- When do I need to respond?
- Is someone trying to persuade/coerce/cajole me into an action or position? If so, what is it, and do I really want to do or think it?
- Am I displaying confirmation bias? Am I really looking at the whole picture?
- Is there any hint of coercion (authority figures, limited availability etc.)?
- What media should I use to respond? (it's best to reply using the same channels – email to email, letter to letter etc).

CONCLUSION

Remember that the intention of the communication needs to be considered. A simple message informing you of something does not often require a response. A more formal message may make a formal response stating that you've received it and will respond in full later a sensible thing to do. It's also simply polite – an underrated aspect of communication in all its forms. If you're going to be rude, make sure it's deliberate and planned. I spend considerable time planning my deliberate rudeness.

7   FEEDBACK

In the context of this book, the term feedback could be restricted to the specific form of communication relating to the passing of information about work performance – be this about a single event (such as a presentation), or over a time-period, such as an annual appraisal. I suggest that feedback is more than a simple one-way, one-off process. Feedback is really important – too important to be left solely to formal appraisals or project-based 'lessons learned' sessions.

Jay W. Forrester – in his paper 'Some basic concepts in system dynamics' – states:

> There is no beginning or end. We live in a complex of nested feedback loops. Every action, every change in nature, is set within a network of feedback loops. Feedback loops are the structures within which all changes occur.[45]

As a term, feedback is mixed. It's not just about giving, it's about receiving. It's a combination of listening and broadcasting. It's also not restricted to formal sessions such as post-project 'lessons learned' gatherings. To be effective it should be almost continual, and it should benefit both sender and receiver.

In their 2014 book *Thanks for the Feedback: The Science and Art of Receiving Feedback Well*,[46] authors Douglas Stone and Sheila Heen argue that there is a common misconception that we should focus on training managers in delivering feedback, and that as a society we've got things backwards. Their book postulates as to why it would be a better investment if we educated those intended to receive feedback rather than those tasked with delivering it.

A further common misconception regarding feedback is that it is purely episodic and delivered in a time-bound framework, such as receiving your annual performance appraisal at work. The classic Deming Plan, Do, Study, Act (PDSA) loop[47] should be a continual process, with the 'check' element being the moment to handle feedback (see Figure 7.1).

---

45 Forrester, J.W. (2009) *Some basic concepts in system dynamics*. Available from https://www.cc.gatech.edu/classes/AY2018/cs8803cc_spring/research_papers/Forrester-SystemDynamics.pdf.

46 Stone, D. and Heen, S. (2014) *Thanks for the Feedback: The Science and Art of Receiving Feedback Well*. New York: Penguin Group USA.

47 https://deming.org/explore/pdsa/.

Figure 7.1 Deming cycle – plan, do, study, act

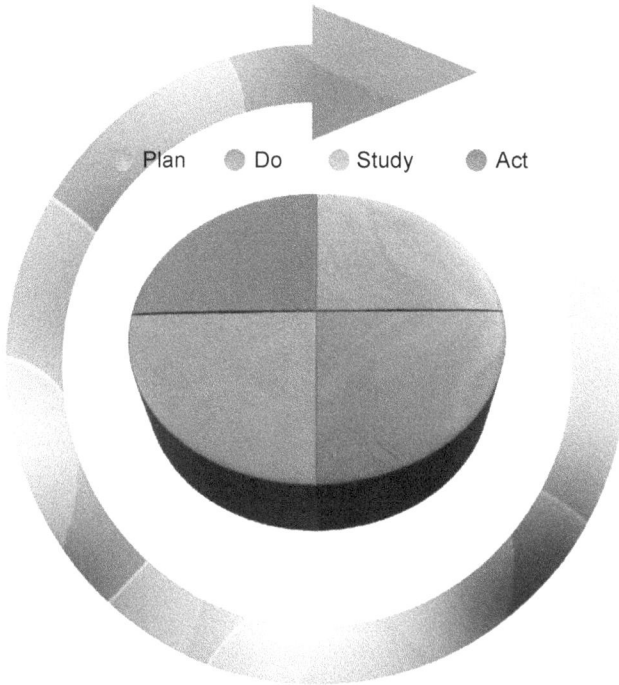

Another reason for avoiding time-bound feedback sessions is that receiving feedback can, in itself, be quite stressful, which is one reason why some people are keen to avoid receiving it. Ed Batista, author of 'Building a feedback-rich culture',[48] stated:

> If you're having a feedback conversation every week, there's less to be surprised by and more opportunity to modify your behavior.

So perhaps we need to teach people how to receive feedback.

FEEDBACK MODELS

There are many models that have been developed to structure how feedback is delivered. Prominent amongst these are:

Situation, Behaviour and Impact (SBI) model™[49]

The SBI model allows employees to take a different perspective from normal, helping them to better to understand any errors or mishaps that may have occurred, and then

---

48 Batista, E. (2013) Building a feedback-rich culture. *Harvard Business Review*, 24 December.

49 https://www.ccl.org/articles/leading-effectively-articles/closing-the-gap-between-intent-vs-impact-sbii/.

discuss strategies they can use for improvement. SBI can be very effective when used for giving rapid feedback responses due to its simplicity.

Sandwich feedback model

The sandwich feedback model intersperses positive feedback with potential areas of improvement – with the areas of improvement 'sandwiched' between positive statements. The approach can help to defuse potentially confrontational meetings and preserves the dignity of those receiving the feedback.

Pendleton feedback model[50]

Pendleton's feedback model focuses on persuading feedback recipients to take a direct role in the feedback process. Just as with the models outlined above, an approach referred to as the sandwich approach also focuses on the positive, whilst ensuring that all participants feel they have been given the chance to air their views.

This method highlights the positive behaviours of the employee, including a discussion on how to achieve these behaviours and any actions that the employee could do differently. By encouraging employees to take an active part in the feedback process, it can help them feel heard while also involving them throughout the process. Here are the seven steps in Pendleton's feedback model:

- making sure that the employee is ready for the feedback;
- allowing the recipient to offer their opinion on the relevant behaviour;
- permitting the recipient to identify what went well;
- allowing the feedback provider to share what they think went well;
- empowering the recipient to outline required improvements;
- permitting the provider to share what they think need to be done;
- both the recipient and provider can agree an improvement plan.

Situation, Task, Action and Result (STAR) feedback model[51]

The STAR model allows the providers to describe a series of events to the recipient, as it can help to ensure that you stay on topic and that your feedback is meaningful. Here is a breakdown of the star method:

- **Situation/Task**

  Explain the relevant task or a situation in detail to the recipient so that all parties understand the context.

---

50 Pendleton, D., Scofield, T., Tate, P. and Havelock, P. (1984) *The Consultation: An Approach to Learning and Teaching.* Oxford: Oxford University Press.

51 https://www.ddiworld.com/solutions/behavioral-interviewing/star-method.

- **Action**

  Provide details about how the recipient handled the situation and what action was taken – no matter if the action resulted in a positive or negative outcome.

- **Result**

  Explain what happened and why it is considered effective or otherwise. This sets out whether the recipient had handled the situation appropriately.

SAID feedback model

The SAID model has four parts – strengths (S), action (A), impact (I) and development (D). Like the other models outlined above, it is designed to help reinforce appropriate behaviour when the feedback is positive, and helps to drive behavioural change when constructive feedback is delivered.

HOW TO GET GOOD FEEDBACK

Good feedback is feedback that provides value. Value can be subjective, but it can include such things as the identification of weaknesses that can be used to identify training needs and support career development. It is normally constructive criticism that provides this value. It may contain personal criticism. It may contain unflattering views on your behaviour. Such things do not make the feedback bad *per se*, and looking solely for positive responses is very likely to be detrimental in the long term. Sheila Heen[52] states 'People who go out and solicit negative feedback — meaning they aren't just fishing for compliments — report higher satisfaction.' She continues 'They adapt more quickly to new roles, get higher performance reviews, and show others they are committed to doing their jobs.'[53]

Seemingly negative feedback can be made positive. The following steps can help you obtain quality, valuable feedback:

1. **Know what you want** – and ask for it. Do you want performance evaluation? General advice? Appreciation and acknowledgement? One thing is essential – you must ask quality questions. Saying 'do you have any feedback for me?' is a waste of breath.

2. **Request feedback as soon as possible** – and also after a brief delay. Rapidity gives a freshness and immediacy to the feedback and is probably more likely to reflect reality. People's memory decays pretty quickly, and it's sensible to capture information whilst people still remember it. That said, it can be worth working in stages, in that a first impression may become tempered in time as people muse on what's been said. In the same way that it's sometimes a good idea to ask for comments after a meeting both immediately after the event **and** ask for responses in slower time. Some people are loath to communicate their thoughts without processing things for a while. The same goes for feedback – you can ask for both.

52 Stone, D. and Heen, S. (2014) *Thanks for the Feedback: The Science and Art of Receiving Feedback Well.* New York: Penguin Group USA.

53 Petriglieri, J., Dowling, D., Harvard Business Review, et al. (2020) *Managing Your Career* (HBR Working Parents Series). Brighton, MA: Harvard Business Review.

3. **Specifics** – the worst kind of feedback is when someone says something like 'seems OK to me' or 'you have to sharpen up your delivery'. General statements like these are vague and essentially useless. Ask for specifics – especially examples. Relating comments to actual events does two things. It helps you (as the feedback-receiver) to better understand what's been said, and secondly, it makes the feedback-giver think more about what they mean, and it will help them to articulate their insights more accurately. I received too many school reports that delivered variations on the phrase 'could do better'. Thanks guys – that's really helpful.

4. '**360 degree feedback**' – one particular aspect of feedback is to recognise that it is not always a 'top-down' approach that works. Some organisations use the term '360 degree feedback' to indicate that you should obtain it from line managers, peers, colleagues and anyone who **you** might be managing. Batista has stated 'You'll get more feedback when you're giving some.'[54] It's worth turning this 360 degree approach into something of a virtuous circle, and use it to the benefit of your colleagues and peers.

It's very clear that there's one skill that is essential for receiving feedback effectively. It's called **listening**. Very often I'm involved in discussions that include a structured exchange of views – with participants taking turns to speak. If emotions become inflamed during these discussions, it's not uncommon for people to start talking over each other and for voices to become louder. Even when this is not happening, many such discussions and conversations involved people waiting to speak – and not listening to what's actually being said. The pauses provide the opportunity to speak – not necessarily based on what's been said. One approach is called active listening.

Active listening

The purpose of active listening (sometimes referred to as empathetic listening) is simple – it's to understand what someone is saying. To make it work requires the listener to focus on what's being said and not use the time to prepare a response. Whilst it can feel counter-intuitive, **not** preparing a response in order to listen will actually improve your response – although it might delay it for a short period. This inevitably requires the listener to practice patience and have the discipline to retain focus. It takes effort – particularly if the subject matter is new, complex or simply bone-dry. Distraction and boredom are the enemy of active listening. It's also sensible and, quite frankly, polite, to try not to multi-task and be distracted by phone calls, texts and emails.

Another approach includes ensuring you understand what's been said by asking open-ended questions. An open-ended question is a question that cannot be answered with a simple 'yes' or 'no' response. A closed-ended question only requires a simple, single response. They have their place (such as testing a person's knowledge) but are little use when trying to understand something complicated.

Examples of open-ended questions include:

- Why did you choose that answer?

---

54 Harvard Business Review (2019) *HBR Guide to Your Professional Growth*. Boston, MA: Harvard Business Press.

- Tell me why you think *x* or *y* is important.
- How do you visualise this process changing in the next year or so?
- Tell me about the process you use to gather the data.
- What is the purpose of sound ethical practice?

A good active listener might also take time to summarise what's been said and repeat this summary back to the speaker to help the listener:

a) organise their thoughts on the subject;

b) confirm their understanding of the subject with the speaker.

It's also worth recalling the statements in Chapter 6 of this book relating to 'confirmation bias'. One states, 'When listening or reading, we all have a tendency to unconsciously select information that supports our point of view.' You must try to put your personal biases aside and be as non-judgemental as is possible. As with so many things in this chapter, this is often counter-intuitive.

There is a final aspect to active listening that will be expanded upon later in this book. You need to demonstrate open, positive and empathetic body language. You need to use eye-contact, lean towards the speaker and face them. Mirroring someone's body language can increase empathy, but can be detrimental if it's done poorly and is spotted by the other party. Glancing over their shoulder, fiddling with your phone and slumping in your chair both reduce the effectiveness of your listening, and will no doubt annoy the speaker – making **them** less effective. It's been suggested that using this approach can improve the quality of voice communications that do not have a visual aspect.

HOW TO GIVE GOOD FEEDBACK

It's worth looking at the steps outlined above regarding how to **get** good feedback. These can be reversed as follows:

1. Make sure the recipient of your feedback knows what they want. If it's unclear, it's worth asking them what they need. You can maybe prompt them with suggestions – especially of you want to investigate some specific areas. This is also important because preparation is essential for both parties. This should not involve a scripted approach, but a few guiding bullets will help. It's also worth making sure you have concrete examples that support your feedback.

2. Although providing rapid feedback is helpful, it is important to remember that feedback can also be provided after a gap in time. There's no magic number to this – a day or so after an event is alright. Anything much over a week means that knowledge and impressions will fade, and the quality of the feedback will do the same.

3. As mentioned earlier, the worst kind of feedback is when someone says something like 'seems OK to me' or 'you have to sharpen up your delivery'. The person to whom you are delivering feedback should, if all's gone well, have advised you of any specific areas they want to discuss – as well as providing examples. You need

to respond in kind, and be specific, give examples and be prepared to answer open-ended questions. Such collaboration and cooperation will improve the feedback session and be valuable to you as well as your colleague.

4. Be prepared to answer questions from people who are junior to you or are your peers. The virtuous 360 degree approach provides the broadest benefit.

One vital aspect of delivering feedback is understanding the difference between constructive and negative feedback. I think it goes – almost without saying – that pure negative feedback is for the most part unhelpful. This is not to suggest that you should never criticise – it's the manner, tone, mode, intent and purpose of the feedback that changes the negative into constructive.

The key differences between negative feedback (aka criticism) and constructive feedback is that whilst both types are intended to challenge you, one tends to be hurtful, whilst the other **should** not. Criticism is often perceived as judgemental, accusatory and detrimental. Constructive feedback is intended to help people help themselves and then grow, rather than to beat them down.

Constructive feedback

Constructive feedback aims to provide a positive outcome through supplying a person with comments, advice or suggestions that are useful for their work or their future. These useful outcomes can include improved timekeeping, higher deliverable quality or better relationships with colleagues. It normally combines positive elements (praise when due) and direct criticism. Both have a part to play.

What is important is to focus on the work or tasks the feedback recipient is involved in or responsible for. Personal criticism is hard to handle and invokes a range of emotions and behaviours that can obstruct your attempts to be positive. Providing initial positive feedback is extremely sensible. It sets the mood for the meeting and can soothe nerves. However – it does contain a potential trap. You can be delivering a stream of positive messages, and then negate them by pausing and then using the word 'but'. This is like a change of tack and can damage the mood and soothing effect you started with, and usher in the negative emotions relating to negative feedback.

Having avoided saying 'but', there has to be a change in approach when dealing with the less positive news. One key factor in this is to ensure that the feedback recipient knows that whatever is said is intended to be constructive, and that that feedback is not about the person – it's about the performance. The intention of the feedback session must be clear.

These sessions require your 'soft skills' as set out in the Introduction – including empathy, listening and awareness of body language. Feeling the mood of the meeting correctly will allow you to temper your tone and language if needed and help to give you an opportunity to reassure the recipient as you proceed. It's worth establishing the purpose of the session and re-establishing it if things become stressed – we all want to do well, and the session is the means by which we all hope we can find a way to help everyone do well. It's about finding solutions, not airing problems.

There are some overarching aspects to delivering feedback. Some are quite specific and seemingly minor – for example, you should make sure that you are not overheard. These sessions should be private. You must be sincere – whilst informality is normally helpful, the importance of the session should be stressed, even if delivered in a friendly manner. You need to be prepared to receive feedback yourself – it's a great opportunity to hear what other people think of you.

Finally – the advice on active listening applies as much to giving feedback as receiving. Feedback, even in a relatively formal session, tends to be a two-way street. It's all part of the virtuous circle.

CONCLUSION

As mentioned in the introduction to this chapter – feedback is really important – too important to be left solely to formal appraisals or project-based 'lessons learned' sessions. Seeking a constant flow of feedback on your performance is part of a virtuous circle, and if it becomes a regular habit, it becomes less worrying through familiarity and will help to make the process more transparent. Transparency tends to lead to honesty, and honesty improves the quality of your communication. It also gives you the opportunity to provide immediate feedback to your colleagues in return, which itself should be mostly positive.

8   COLLABORATION

WHY COLLABORATE?

Collaboration (from Latin *com-* 'with' + *laborare-* 'to work') is the process by which groups of people, teams or organisations work together to achieve a common task or goal. Collaboration is one of the main reasons why we, a small, hairless, clawless, virtually toothless ape species, have been able to dominate a world inhabited by large, hairy, betoothed and beclawed beasts.

In around 370 BCE a former student of Socrates called Xenephon wrote a semi-biographic history of the founder of the Persian Empire – Cyrus the Great – called *The Cyropaedia* – also referred to as 'The Education of Cyrus'. The book has been widely channelled across the years, not least by Machiavelli with his famous discourse on leadership called *The Prince*.[55] One statement in the Cyropaedia stands out as follows:

> social bonds, not command and control, were to be the primary mechanisms of governance.

Note that, in my opinion, the concept of command and control (C&C) is pretty much dead. Perhaps it always was. It might have worked briefly in many circumstances, but societies and organisations that try to operate on a strict C&C basis tend to be short-lived, brutish and doomed. Even the Roman Empire was essentially a collaborative trading bloc. It may have been brutal in conquest, but this changed once a territory was taken, and local peoples assimilated into the Empire. Newly incorporated Roman citizens enjoyed the benefits of this vast conglomerate (because that was what it was). It could only happen through collaboration. It's worth looking at the works of Peter Drucker, Tom Peters and Douglas McGregor to better understand that C&C has a place within most organisations – but it should be limited and short-lived – and only employed at times of great need. Dictatorships tend to die an early and rather nasty death.

---

55 Machiavelli, N.B. (1515) *The Prince.*

WHAT IS COLLABORATION?

The best example of collaboration is trade. Trade is a form of collaboration between two societies that produce different things and can exchange them for things they can't get or make themselves. For example, tin was an extremely important metal historically because it allowed the production of bronze – a hard-wearing metal suitable for tools and weapons. The tin mines in Cornwall traded their precious metal across Europe – items containing Cornish tin have been found in Scandinavia, what is now modern Germany, and off the coast of Haifa in Israel. The tin was traded for luxury goods – notably during the Roman era.

Bringing this dialogue into the modern world – the purest form of collaboration has to involve parties 'self-organising' – much in the same way ancient traders would have had to operate. In 2001, a group of software developers met and began the process of creating the 'Manifesto for Agile Software Development' – known as 'The Agile Manifesto'.[56] The Manifesto focuses on 12 principles. These are:

1. Our highest priority is to satisfy the customer through early and continuous delivery of valuable software.
2. Welcome changing requirements, even late in development. Agile processes harness change for the customer's competitive advantage.
3. Deliver working software frequently, from a couple of weeks to a couple of months, with a preference to the shorter timescale.
4. Business people and developers must **work together daily throughout the project**.
5. Build projects around motivated individuals. Give them the environment and support they need, and trust them to get the job done.
6. The most efficient and effective method of conveying information to and within a development team is **face-to-face conversation**.
7. Working software is the primary measure of progress.
8. Agile processes promote sustainable development. The sponsors, developers, and users should be able to maintain a constant pace indefinitely.
9. Continuous attention to technical excellence and good design enhances agility.
10. Simplicity–the art of maximizing the amount of work not done–is essential.
11. **The best architectures, requirements, and designs emerge from self-organizing teams.**
12. At regular intervals, the team reflects on how to become more effective, then tunes and adjusts its behavior accordingly.

It is principle number 11 that captures my attention in this context.

---

56 See https://agilemanifesto.org/.

The introduction to the Manifesto states:

> We are uncovering better ways of developing software by doing it and helping others do it. Through this work we have come to value:
>
>> Individuals and interactions over processes and tools
>> Working software over comprehensive documentation
>> **Customer collaboration** over contract negotiation
>> Responding to change over following a plan
>
> That is, while there is value in the items on the right, we value the items on the left more.

I have highlighted those terms and phrases that indicate that the Agile movement knows and understands the necessity for collaboration. It is not for show. It's modern, fresh, yet rooted in antiquity.

COLLABORATION CULTURE

One of the best-known analyses of different cultures that influence collaboration was performed and published by an American social psychologist called Douglas McGregor who proposed a theory in his 1960 book *The Human Side of Enterprise* that outlined two contrasting belief systems known as Theory X and Theory Y. Theory X is based on the mindset that people didn't want to work and had to be coerced. Theory Y suggests a mindset that people are keen, collaborative and self-starting.[57]

Echoes of this contrast are heard in discussions on remote working (or 'working from home') that evolved during and after the COVID-19 pandemic. These discussions are exacerbated by further debate on the effectiveness of reducing the working week from five to four days. It seems (according to current analysis) that remote and 'hybrid' working is, at the very worst, as effective as a full-time office-based approach. Most analysis suggests it provides additional efficiency, and it also seems that the four-day week is proving better than a five-day week in terms of overall productivity. This might seem to be a victory for Theory Y.

Theory Y can be described as 'participatory', avoids coercion and C&C, and suggests most people actually thrive on an open collaborative culture. Theory Y suggests that work is an inbuilt part of humanity, and that people love to collaborate, use their imagination and demonstrate their creative abilities.

Based on the above, a Theory X manager or supervisor is driven by the following. They believe that people:

- dislike work;
- avoid responsibility and need continual direction;

---

57 McGregor, D. and Cutcher-Gershenfeld, J.E. (2008) *The Human Side of Enterprise*. New York: McGraw Hill Professional.

- need to be controlled, coerced and threatened to deliver work;
- require to be supervised at every step;
- have neither ambition nor incentive to work, and need to be enticed to achieve goals.

Characteristics of managers using Theory X include:

- results-based focus;
- independent operation;
- provide limited feedback, and do not ask for feedback;
- regular scrutiny of teamwork;
- process efficiency rated highly;
- deadline oriented;
- limited delegation and decision making.

Examples of Theory X managerial behaviours include:

- arrogant, detached and distant;
- delegates risk to juniors, but never the rewards;
- has a short fuse that manifests through shouting and aggression;
- has no concern for staff welfare, and never gives out praise or offers thanks;
- has no empathy with staff, and thinks morale is irrelevant;
- has no interest in participatory and team-oriented work styles;
- is a cheapskate, both in terms of salaries and the awarding of expenses;
- issues ultimatums (often using deadlines);
- manages through impractical deadlines and deliverables, often to no good purpose;
- never makes a request, but will issue a demand;
- obsessive dedication to results and deadlines, even when they are seen over time to be not in the best interest of the organisation;
- operates a 'blame' culture, often looking for 'the guilty party' (failing to learn from mistakes in the process);
- operates in 'broadcast' mode most of the time – is rarely in 'receive' mode;
- operates via orders, instructions and threats;
- poor at investing in future success;
- snobbish and overly proud – sometimes elitist;
- unable to tolerate outsiders and people who disagree;

- will retain the ownership of the benefits of work (such as bonuses) but will shed accountability onto junior staff;
- will retaliate against people who criticise them, and will fail to take suggestions.

Whilst the above may seem to be deeply unfair to those who follow the Theory X path, there's little doubt that in most circumstances a full Theory X approach is less effective than Theory Y. The core reason for this is that collaboration and communication are the keys to successful delivery. It's normally only in extreme cases that Theory X is appropriate. These include wartime combat, search and rescue, and massively compressed delivery timescales.

Two further concepts that are closely related to the above are **conformity** and **compliance**. These describe two different ways in which people are motivated – much like Theory X and Theory Y.

Conformity tends to be driven from within an individual, such as wanting to contribute to a group effort or initiative. Many of the elements within conformity are essentially subconscious. Compliance tends to be externally imposed, often in parallel with a reward scheme or a regime of punishment. People comply because they feel they must, or consider the price (financial, emotional, social etc.) as being too high. **Compliance** requires reporting and policing. This can be expensive, time-consuming and potentially counter-productive. Conformity has hidden inbuilt costs, and requires vigilance and awareness, but the approach is better suited for achieving the 'self-organising' ideas set out in the Agile Manifesto.

Another concept that needs examination is that of '**organisational health**'. A key element of a healthy organisation is one that succeeds in achieving its goals. If you are still seeking further evidence to answer the question 'Why collaborate?', it's worth delving into the world on Monty Python. John Cleese wrote a book in collaboration with the psychiatrist Robin Skynner called *Life and How to Survive It*. In this book they spent some considerable time talking about the 'health' of organisations. They suggested that a healthy organisation had some specific characteristics as follows:

- trust;
- openness;
- a tolerance for independence;
- being allowed to make mistakes.[58]

Skynner and Cleese conclude that a healthy organisation is more likely to make money than an unhealthy one. Poor communication and collaboration is often detectable in an organisation by such elements as a 'blame culture'. If you **know** you are going to be blamed in the event of a mistake (whether it's your fault or not), one of the most natural reactions is to do one thing – cover things up and block the communications flow. This can become endemic in an organisation and all communications can become muted and muffled. Without a decent information flow, you cannot operate effectively.

---

58 Skynner, R. and Cleese, J. (1997) *Life and How to Survive It*. New York: Norton.

In an unhealthy organisation, one of the first things you will detect is poor information flow. People are too scared to report events. If they cannot block the flow, they often distort the evidence through change and omission to avoid blame or to pass it on to someone else. Poor information flow results in poor decisions, potentially illegal reporting (especially if the distortion is made on financial information) and can form a self-reinforcing negative spiral that feeds on itself and becomes totally entrenched.

CONCLUSION

Collaboration is a group effort. It begins with people deciding to involve other people in their work. It's very clear that one of the key attributes needed to make this work is simple – it's trust. Trust involves letting people make decisions for themselves. It involves people accepting when they get things wrong – and not passing the blame. It is not a panacea – it can go wrong and make things worse, but this is rare. Even less successful collaboration attempts are better than stony silence.

Supporting this collaborative ideal is also simple – clear communication is essential. Leadership involves gaining trust, communicating clearly and delivering results. This should set up what could be deemed a 'virtuous circle'. We've already discussed a 'a self-reinforcing negative spiral that feeds on itself' – the opposite what is needed. Team-based self-organisation coupled with delegating decision making to the **real** experts is more effective than bullying instructions and orders.

It's worth looking at the thinking on collaboration and communication provided by Peter Drucker.

After years of consultancy experience at large organisations such as IBM, General Motors and Procter & Gamble, Drucker wrote *The Practice of Management*[59] in 1954. He outlined a then-revolutionary approach to management that was holistic and multi-disciplinary. He also outlined the concepts of management-by-objectives and SMART[60] thinking.

Drucker recommended that managers should 'lead' rather than 'manage' and preferred a creative approach as opposed to bureaucratic management. One revolutionary idea was to avoid setting strict hours – perhaps anticipating working from home and a four-day week. What he truly aimed for was a flexible, collaborative approach.

It's plain that people need to share ideas and communicate clearly. Setting up colleagues in opposition to each other rarely provides results. There's little wrong with individual work when it's appropriate, but collaboration is the crux and centre of a successful way forward.

---

[59] Drucker, P. (1954) *The Practice of Management*. New York: Harper & Row.

[60] SMART goals or objectives are specific, measurable, achievable, relevant and time-bound.

9   COLLABORATION TOOLS

It is easy to be seduced by the plethora of tools and apps available to assist collaboration. There are many more basic approaches that are essential and depend on little more than decency and thoughtfulness. These range from the seemingly casual, such as being polite and answering questions in a timely manner, to those that are more theoretical and process driven. Many of these are covered in this book, but it's worth listing a few. They should include:

- be kind;
- be on time;
- listen, and respond when asked with clarity;
- be truthful.

Remember, a fool with a tool is still a fool. Simple practices are of great value and include internal team collaboration meetings wherein one can recognise improvements and successes. This can also be achieved via team-building events and informal learning opportunities such as 'lunch and learn' sessions. The important thing is to encourage ideas and discuss them in a blame-free and open environment.

This section is written with the assumption that the tools in question are mostly online apps, programs or platforms that are designed to increase team productivity, support creativity and keep everyone in the team up to date with the status of deliverables, project progress and team members' location and availability. These tools help team leaders and members assign tasks, provide update reports and manage team workflow. Most of the collaboration platforms provide communication channels as well – all integrated into a single entity.

There is no set series of characteristics that define a collaboration tool. There's a danger when listing specific examples of tools in a book that the list will go out of date as soon as the book goes to print, but it's worth listing a few of the more visible and common ones as examples. These include project management applications, remote conferencing platforms and messaging apps. Some people use the term 'groupware' to describe collaboration platforms. Such platforms provide services like those listed below:

- Document collaboration systems – allowing multiple people to edit and update a single document to produce an agreed (and version tracked) deliverable. This includes centralised storage for documents, images, audio, videos and multiple other file types. It can include features such as instant messaging and integration with time management systems – helping schedule events and provide team members with reminders. These systems are normally integrated with online diaries provided by applications such as MS Outlook.

- Project management support – tracking project milestones, activities and deliverables.
- Workflow support.
- Knowledge management such as an interactive dashboard capable of displaying status on tasks, workflow, milestones, decisions and team members.
- Remote learning and meeting platforms.

The platform needs to be appropriately secure to provide privacy for personal data and protection of any other sensitive information – particularly if one operates in sectors that are impacted by relevant regulation and legislation. These sectors can include government and any organisation handling personally identifiable information (PII) as defined under the General Data Protection Regulation (GDPR).

COMMON COLLABORATION TOOLS AND SUITES

MS SharePoint

One of the most commonly used platforms is MS SharePoint. SharePoint is specifically designed to integrate with Microsoft Office. It provides a range of services including document management, but can also handle the development of intranet content, deliver questionnaires and collaborative software. It is highly configurable and given its tight integration with MS products, it can utilise Outlook, Word, Excel, OneDrive and Project to handle input, storage and delivery. It can also be used to deliver information via a wiki – helping onboard new team members by centralising corporate and project information. Its core strength is that it can enable the managed storage, retrieval, search, archiving, tracking and reporting of online documents and similar records.

Google Workspace

Google Workspace is a suite of cloud computing, productivity and collaboration tools, software and products. It includes Gmail, Contacts, Calendar, Meet and Chat. It uses the Google Docs Editors suite for content creation, which is freeware available to anyone with a personal Google account. It can be delivered via a web app, various mobile (Android and iOS) apps, and directly via Google's ChromeOS. It is connected to the Google Drive service that provides cloud-based storage. It allows for collaborative editing of documents and can handle most MS Office file formats – and it constituent services (Docs, Sheets, Slides, Drawings, Forms and so forth) provide capability approximately equivalent to the MS Office tools. It is also available as an enterprise-level offering that can include custom email addresses and additional support and tools.

Atlassian

Atlassian have developed collaborative tools that integrate with other products to support teams. One offering, Confluence, using a similar approach to SharePoint and Google Workspace, works in conjunction with related Atlassian software products such as Jira (which supports bug tracking and agile project management), as well as other offerings called Bamboo, Clover, Crowd, Crucible and Fisheye.wiki.

HOW TO CHOOSE A COLLABORATION TOOL

Choosing a tool is much the same as any purchase. An early priority is cost. The beauty of many of the collaboration tools and suites is that they are free. The freeware normally comes with a limited option set, with additional features being made available on purchasing various levels of licence. It's all down to what you're prepared to pay. The same issues relate to product support – the more you pay, the better it tends to get.

Perhaps the best route is to take up a freeware offer and see how you get on with it. The following list is a series of tool sets that are prominent – I'm making no calls or judgement as to how good they are, or if they're still in business when this book goes to print.

- Asana;
- Confluence;
- Google Docs;
- Huddle;
- Jira;
- MS 365;
- Teams;
- Trello;
- Zoom.

The following list sets out some of the additional potential facilities one might expect from a collaboration tool:

- brainstorming;
- chat;
- conferencing;
- meeting management;
- mind mapping;
- process documents;

- project management;

- whiteboards.

What may be important is the corporate tools you already have in place. Most organisations use MS or the Apple equivalent – so it may be worth making sure your chosen suite can integrate with them.

Rather than committing to print with a list of options, a very useful online reference is provided by Wikipedia – https://en.wikipedia.org/wiki/List_of_collaborative_software.

10 ANALYSING YOUR COLLABORATION SKILLS

INTRODUCTION

Much of what is written about communication and collaboration centres on the way in which one delivers messages and how you project yourself. These are important, but there is another factor in this that is as essential and as true. If you know how you are perceived, it gives you the means to tailor your delivery and your messages to become more effective. If you know yourself, it allows you to disclose aspects of your personality and ideas – which in turn can help build trust.

JOHARI MODEL

Finding out about yourself can take time, involve self-learning, reflection, therapy, foreign travel and introspection. I don't have enough time for that so thought I would set out a means to help self-discovery along. This is the Johari Window Model (see Figure 10.1).[61] The model was developed by two psychologists, Joseph Luft and Harry Ingham, who smashed their names together to create the name 'Johari' in 1955. It provides a framework that can help people understand their conscious and unconscious bias and thereby assist self-awareness and awareness of others.

It provides a straightforward means for anyone to examine their personality, and through this, facilitate understanding between people and groups. It can be used for many purposes – notably improving collaboration in the workplace.

The model consists of four quadrants in which users can:

- identify what they know about themselves; and
- identify what other people know about them.

The technique used involves a list of adjectives that describe a person's personality. Some sources state that there are 55 adjectives – others that there are 56. Suffice

---

61 Luft, J. and Ingham, H. (1955) The Johari Window, a graphic model of interpersonal awareness. In *Proceedings of the Western Training Laboratory in Group Development*. Los Angeles: UCLA.

Figure 10.1 Johari Window Model[62]

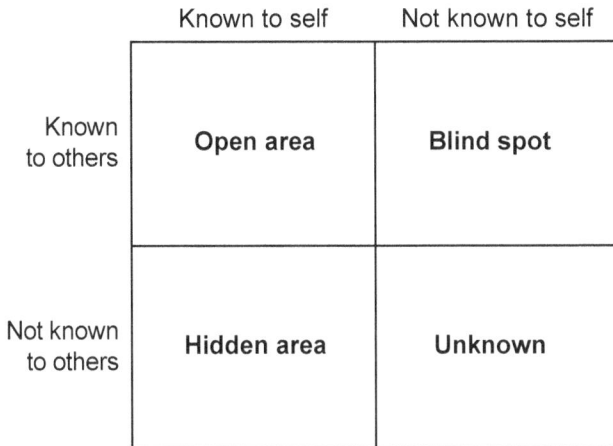

	Known to self	Not known to self
Known to others	**Open area**	**Blind spot**
Not known to others	**Hidden area**	**Unknown**

to say, there are quite a lot of them. The following list of 57 seems to have broad acceptance:[63]

Able, accepting, adaptable, bold, brave, calm, caring, cheerful, clever, complex, confident, dependable, dictate, empathetic, energetic, extroverted, friendly, giving, happy, helpful, idealistic, independent, ingenious, intelligent, introverted, kind, knowledgeable, logical, loving, mature, modest, nervous, observant, organised, patient, powerful, proud, quiet, reflective, relaxed, religious, responsive, searching, self-assertive, self-conscious, sensible, sentimental, shy, silly, smart, spontaneous, sympathetic, tense, trustworthy, warm, wise, witty.

The method requires that the subject of the analysis (let's call them 'you') selects adjectives you feel describe your personality. Your peers select the same number of adjectives from the same list that they feel describe you. The words are then placed into a 2×2 grid of four boxes. The four boxes can be displayed as a picture that looks a bit like a window.

The four boxes (or quadrants) are:

Open

If you **and** your peers select the same adjective, it goes into this box. The 'open' quadrant covers your inner consciousness – those elements (as described by the adjectives) that you know about, and that other people are likely to know about.

---

62 Ibid.

63 I did find a wonderfully warped version of the technique called 'Nohari', which seeks to use negative adjectives to disclose character flaws. Adjectives included insecure, intolerant and violent.

These include your principles, values, assertions, drivers and attitudes. We all tend to be fairly comfortable in this space.

Façade/hidden

This quadrant is normally not known by your peers. Generally, only you know about these elements, so those adjectives you have chosen but your peers have **not** go into this box.

Blind spot

If your peers select an adjective but you do **not**, it goes into this box. These represent what others perceive but you don't.

Unknown

If an adjective is **not** chosen by you or your peers it goes into this box. These are aspects of you that no one participating recognises – normally because they don't apply – although they may be hidden for a variety of reasons.

The model is not a fully empirical means to obtain exact psychological data. It can be described as a means to get everybody 'on the same page'. Over time, it would be beneficial for each person who uses the model to extend the 'Open' window as far as possible in terms of the group they work with.

If your own personal foibles are visible, well-known and understood, the more likely it is that communication will improve. If a team undertakes the exercise, and expand their own 'Open' areas, the effect is multiplied. It's also very good at improving self-awareness, which in turn should improve how individuals operate.

A key objective of the process is to develop the Open area for all participants. It's in this quadrant that quality communications can take place, and this should have a corresponding positive impact on such welcome things as productivity. The area is where negative elements such as mistrust, conflict and misunderstanding are least likely to manifest.

When dealing with a team, it is obvious that those members who are well embedded will have larger Open areas than newcomers – mainly because it is inevitable that limited personal information is shared at this stage by a newcomer. As time goes on, and the Johari process is repeated, what was initially in other areas will, through personal disclosure, discussion and other forms of feedback, transfer into the Open area.

The Blind spot area needs to be reduced over time, and this reduction is compensated by the positive expansion of the Open area. It is neither a productive nor effective space, and can relate to some very negative aspects, including self-delusion, deliberate exclusion and the withholding of information. Discussion and feedback relating to this area needs care and sensitivity.

The Hidden area also requires some thought and sensitivity. There are often good reasons why people hide thoughts, feelings and fears. The purpose of the Johari approach is to reveal those elements that are work-related, and to expand the Open area to improve communication – and thereby increase the positive benefits already discussed. Many people feel concerned that revealing these elements can make them vulnerable or open to ridicule – which is why the process needs management and care.

Discovering the Unknown elements is not subject to a rigid process. Capabilities, thoughts, insights and skills can be unearthed via a multitude of means. They can emerge under stress, such as during an emergency, or when someone is asked to perform a task they are not familiar with, or use a tool that they've never used before. Unknown elements can become clear during phases of self-discovery and introspection. What is important is that they are shared, and that they be moved as cleanly as possible into the Open area.

It's clear from the above that the Johari process is not a single event. In needs to be run periodically, or for specific events such as new team members arriving. It allows you to know yourself, know others and to let others know you.

CONCISENESS

You have no idea how tempted I was to write 'conciseness is a communications technique eliminating redundant words' and leave it at that. However, it's never as easy as that. Being concise (or succinct, or laconic) takes effort, thought and time.

It takes time to be precise, but it's time worth spending. Joseph M. Williams, an English language and literature professor at the University of Chicago published a book called *Style: Ten Lessons in Clarity and Grace* in 1981.[64] It's based on a course Williams taught, and lesson seven is called 'Concision'. He sets out six principles as follows:

- Delete words that mean little or nothing.
- Delete words that repeat the meaning of other words.
- Delete words implied by other words.
- Replace a phrase with a word.
- Change negatives to affirmatives.
- Delete useless adjectives and adverbs.

Prior to Williams, another American English language professor, William Strunk Jr., wrote *The Elements of Style* in 1918.[65] The book underwent significant modification by others, notably E.B. White, who revised and expanded the book as co-author in 1959.[66]

---

[64] Williams, J.M. (1981) *Style: Ten Lessons in Clarity and Grace*. Glenview, IL: Scott Foresman.

[65] Strunk Jr., W. (1918) *The Elements of Style*. New York: Harcourt, Brace and Company.

[66] Strunk Jr., W. (1959) *The Elements of Style … with Revisions, an Introduction, and a New Chapter on Writing by White, E.B.* New York: Macmillan.

Strunk states in section 13 of the 1918 version 'Omit needless words':

> Vigorous writing is concise. A sentence should contain no unnecessary words, a paragraph no unnecessary sentences, for the same reason that a drawing should have no unnecessary lines and a machine no unnecessary parts. This requires not that the writer make all his sentences short, or that he avoid all detail and treat his subjects only in outline, but that he make every word tell. ('Elementary Principles of Composition', *The Elements of Style*)

This is obviously not a new issue. The astoundingly capable French writer, mathematician and philosopher Blaise Pascal stated in a letter written in 1657:[67]

> *Je n'ai fait celle-ci plus longue que parce que je n'ai pas eu le loisir de la faire plus courte.*
> (I only made this one longer because I didn't have time to make it shorter.)

I was taught the art of precis at school as part of my GCE English Language O Level (note the GCE – this is pre-GCSE stuff – I'm really old). The technique was surprisingly simple but has helped me all my working life. It's a four-step process as follows:

- Write the sentence/paragraph/report section text as normal.
- Review your text carefully.
- Highlight any truly meaningful words.
- Rewrite your text by focusing on the meaningful words.

What do I mean by meaningful? It's worth looking at how some words are **not** meaningful. In an article in *The New York Times* from 23 July 2012, Helen Sword wrote about what she terms 'zombie nouns':

> Take an adjective (implacable) or a verb (calibrate) or even another noun (crony) and add a suffix like ity, tion or ism. You've created a new noun: implacability, calibration, cronyism. Sounds impressive, right?

> Nouns formed from other parts of speech are called nominalizations. Academics love them; so do lawyers, bureaucrats and business writers. I call them 'zombie nouns' because they cannibalize active verbs, suck the lifeblood from adjectives and substitute abstract entities for human beings.[68]

Sword uses an example from George Orwell, author of *1984*, wherein he 'translates' a passage from Ecclesiastes in the King James version of the Bible into contemporary English. The original is as follows:

> I returned and saw under the sun, that the race is not to the swift, nor the battle to the strong, neither yet bread to the wise, nor yet riches to men of understanding, nor yet favour to men of skill; but time and chance happeneth to them all.

---

[67] From a series of letters known as *Les Provinciales* (1656–1657).

[68] Sword, H. (2012) *Zombie nouns*. The New York Times. Available from https://archive.nytimes.com/opinionator.blogs. nytimes.com/2012/07/23/zombie-nouns/.

Here it is in modern English:

Objective considerations of contemporary phenomena compel the conclusion that success or failure in competitive activities exhibits no tendency to be commensurate with innate capacity, but that a considerable element of the unpredictable must invariably be taken into account.[69]

If your text is less clear and engaging than text commissioned in 1604 and published in 1611 by King James then you really are in trouble. I have taken Orwell's 'modern English' and used the four step process I outlined above:

Objective considerations of contemporary phenomena compel the conclusion that **success** or **failure** in competitive activities exhibits **no tendency** to be commensurate with **innate capacity**, but that a considerable element of the **unpredictable** must **invariably** be taken into account.

This results in a very simple but impactful phrase:

Success and failure are as dependent on luck as on ability.

You will need to absorb the lessons set out by Williams, Strunk and White, and apply them using the simple four step process. You will need to make sure you understand the purpose and context of the text you are addressing, especially if it is aimed at a specialist or select readership. It may of course be important to address issues relating to jargon and other matters discussed in Chapter 1. Conciseness, clarity, lack of ambiguity and precision all form part of the process of communication and collaboration. Your skill set needs to be broad and takes input from many sources. There is no panacea.

ASSERTIVENESS

Assertiveness is seen when a person affirms their position or viewpoint without being aggressive whilst ensuring they do not act in a submissive manner that may cause them to be ignored or denied.

Assertiveness is important. Clear communication of wishes and boundaries is essential, but the process should never descend into anger or similar emotional outbursts if your wishes are not met. It allows you to approach other people to request resources or assistance whilst standing up for yourself (or your colleagues) in a non-aggressive way. It can also protect them from bullies and other social predators.

Assertiveness is not always an innate God-given trait – it can be learned and used effectively. Many of the techniques that can be learned have emerged from cognitive behavioural therapy (CBT) as a way of helping people manage issues such as depression. It's clear that being able to assert yourself not only makes you a better, more effective communicator, but it can also boost your mental health.

---

69 Orwell, G. (1946) *Politics and the English Language*. London: Horizon.

There is no single reference for these methods and techniques, but the most commonly cited are:

- basic assertion;
- empathic assertion;
- consequence assertion;
- discrepancy technique;
- repetition technique (sometime called the broken record technique);
- fogging technique.

Basic assertion

This approach is straightforward. Work out exactly what you want, and then tell those who need to know in a clear, unambiguous manner. It can also be a straightforward statement when standing up for your personal feelings, opinions or rights. There is an aspect of basic assertion that links back to aspects of disclosure in the Johari Window Model set out above. You can disclose some personal aspects of yourself in such straightforward statements – such as, when requested to undertake an additional piece of work at 5.00 p.m. on a Friday – 'I am annoyed that you asked me to do this so late in the day.' You can follow this up with 'I have made plans for this evening and cancelling them will inconvenience a lot of people, so I will not do as you ask.' Some people refer to such disclosure as 'I' statements.

Empathic assertion

Basic assertion is essentially self-centred but assertion is not about dominance or 'victory'. It is important to listen actively and understand and recognise the other person's feelings and needs. Your approach can be made more effective if you recognise and broadcast that you recognise another's needs. I have worked in organisations that had been extremely reluctant to provide costs for any piece of work without extensive internal consultation and governance. This can be frustrating for both you and your clients if what they want is a rapid, rough cost estimate. You will probably have to be assertive in both directions – with your colleagues in an attempt to get them to provide a 'ball-park' number, and with your client to help them understand that such things take time. You have to recognise the drivers and constraints on each party. You can say to your client, for example 'I know you need this information rapidly, but we have internal processes we have to follow, and I'm working on getting you your numbers as quickly as I can.' You could express to colleagues the reverse – 'I know we have these processes, and that they are well-proven, but I have an opportunity here that needs a rapid response. I want the estimate today.'

A word of caution – being empathetic is not just the use of the right words. There are only so many times you can hear terms like 'I hear what you're saying' and 'I feel your pain' before they begin to lose their credibility and efficacy. You have to actually mean it, otherwise your well-chosen empathic opening gambit just becomes a 'noise'.

Consequence assertion

Consequence assertion is the next rung on the ladder. There is a clear escalation path in these techniques – but any drift towards aggression should be spotted and dealt with before you lose your temper – however tempting that might be.

You need to state clearly that there are consequences for not doing as requested. You should only do this when you have the authority to deliver a sanction or similar action, and you need to carry them out if the situation does not change. Making empty threats or failing to carry one out makes your position vulnerable and you become 'noise'. The kind of statement you might use could be, 'I asked you for those numbers for the estimate and you have not provided them, despite the fact we are potentially going to lose an important customer. I'd rather not, but I will escalate this to the head of sales and marketing and to your director unless you help me out.'

Another word of warning – this approach can easily drift into aggression – by both sides in the discussion. It's worth making sure you reduce the chances of this by ensuring your verbal tone and physical posture are not confrontational (body language matters in these situations), and that you always remain open to others' needs and concerns.

Discrepancy technique

The discrepancy technique involves gently mentioning or reminding a person when there appears to be a difference between a current position and one that had been agreed beforehand. Such discrepancies can be the root cause of the need for assertion and have to be handled carefully in that it is often possible to be seen as an accuser – which drifts into bullying and aggression territory – the very state we want to avoid.

You might have to discuss such matters in a guarded but assertive manner as follows: 'Last week you mentioned that safety was our highest priority. It seems from your actions this week that you had downgraded some of the safety work we discussed. Have I misunderstood something or has there been a change I've not been made aware of?' Dialogue has to be open and clear, but avoiding aggression remains key.

Repetition technique

This approach is often termed the 'broken record' approach. In May 1997 there was a very famous political interview between Michael Howard, a politician who had recently left a post in the UK government that included the management of the Prison Service, and the legendary Jeremy Paxman, a BBC interviewer of great repute. Paxman asked Howard the same question relating to the Prison Service 12 times, interspersed with supporting phrases that included, 'With respect, you haven't answered the question.' – 'I'm going to be frightfully rude.' – and 'I note you are not answering the question.'

This approach is not subtle – it's even been described as the demonic opposite of empathic. It can work, but the longer it goes on, the more your repetition becomes 'noise'. This approach is normally best left to Paxman and his fellows, although there may be time when it's the **only** way.

Fogging technique

Fogging is an interesting approach that plays back something that's been said to you that has some element of truth to it. It's useful for diffusing an aggressive situation in that it allows you, to some degree, to agree with your discussion partner. It avoids the 'how dare you' approach to conversation by changing tack slightly and helping you say, for example, 'I know the governance rules on procurement are in place, and we have good reason for using them but we need to provide this information quickly.' You 'fog' the conversation by allying with your partner – especially when they are right – but then loop back to the matter in hand. It relates closely to the empathic approach, in that you are looking to understand other people's points of view.

CONCLUSION

We humans are successful because we collaborate. We all have our strengths and weaknesses, and it is the combination of skills that has allowed us to take over the planet despite us being a weak, small, slow, toothless, clawless and relatively hairless mammal. Failure to collaborate makes us less capable collectively, and we should be seeking to do so whenever possible. It's well worth assessing your own collaboration skills to see how best you can support collaborative ventures.

11 EMOTIONAL INTELLIGENCE AND COLLABORATION

In 1990, Peter Salovey and John Mayer published an article in *Imagination, Cognition and Personality*, an academic publication that presents work that focuses on cognition and mental simulation, subjective aspects of personality, and consciousness.

The article was called 'Emotional intelligence'. In it, Salovey and Mayer describe emotional intelligence (henceforth EI) as 'the ability to monitor one's own and other's emotions, to discriminate among them, and to use the information to guide one's thinking and actions'.[70] They weren't the first to investigate this area – Edward Thorndike (an American psychologist who worked and taught at Teachers College, Columbia University) published work on 'social intelligence'[71] as early as 1920. Others, such as Howard Gardner, a developmental psychologist at Harvard University, postulated a theory of 'multiple intelligence', arguing that intelligence includes eight forms:

- musical;
- visual-spatial;
- linguistic;
- logical-mathematical;
- bodily-kinaesthetic;
- interpersonal;
- intrapersonal;
- naturalistic.[72]

It's clear that EI forms a significant element within a number of the above, notably interpersonal and intrapersonal. There are many essential components of a capable collaborator, such as social capability, emotional flexibility and sensitivity, empathy and self-control. All these characteristics form part of EI.

Salovey and Mayer's work came to prominence through another psychologist – Daniel Goleman – through his book *Emotional Intelligence*. Goleman has gone on to publish

---

70 Salovey, P. and Mayer, J. (1990) Emotional intelligence. *Imagination, Cognition and Personality*, 9 (3), March.

71 Thorndike, E.L. (1920) Intelligence and its uses. *Harper's Magazine*, 14. 227–235.

72 Gardner, H. (1983) *Frames of Mind: The Theory of Multiple Intelligences*. New York: Basic Books.

extensively in this area and postulates that non-cognitive skills (such as EI) can matter as much as IQ in a team and business context. He set out the following four stages of EI.[73]

SELF-AWARENESS

Self-awareness is the ability to understand your own strengths and weaknesses, whilst realising the effect your own emotions have on you – and ultimately – others. It seems that self-awareness is less common than most people perceive. Most people think they are self-aware when the truth is that only 10 to 15 per cent really are.[74] It seems that a lack of self-awareness can reduce team effectiveness by 50 per cent.[75]

The need to be self-aware was discussed in Chapter 10 in relation to the Johari Window Model. There are other approaches you can take, including becoming involved in appraisal practices such as '360 degree feedback', wherein you seek feedback from peers, your direct reports and your line management. There are even simpler methods, such as actually listening to what someone is saying rather than waiting for someone to stop talking so that you can make your point (see the section on active listening in Chapter 7).

SELF-MANAGEMENT

I have a simple technique for improving my email communications. I use it when I'm really, **really** angry with someone, and feel the need to tell them exactly what I think in an email. I write the email text quickly and fully, but do not put anyone's name in the 'To' field. I sometimes do my writing in OneNote or Notepad to prevent me accidentally sending a message. I then leave the text – normally overnight if possible. I then rewrite the email – erasing all the swearing and biological obscenities. The same approach can be done on shorter timescales, such as during spoken conversations, or during SMS and MS Teams message exchanges. The only difference is that you must work more quickly and not let your immediate reaction cause damage. Your response should be measured, truthful and helpful. A tirade rarely solves a problem.

If you found yourself on the verge of a rant, stop. Pause. Think. Calm down. Now you can respond.

SOCIAL AWARENESS

The first two stages relate for the most part to understanding yourself. Understanding other people is the other side of this coin. This book makes almost constant reference to the concept of empathy, and using this alongside the ability to walk in another

---

73 Goleman, D. (1995) *Emotional Intelligence: Why It Can Matter More Than IQ*. New York: Bantam Books

74 Eurich, T. (2018) *Working with people who aren't self-aware*. Harvard Business Review, 19 October. Available from https://hbr.org/2018/10/working-with-people-who-arent-self-aware.

75 Ibid.

person's shoes and recognise their own emotional state is probably more important than understanding your own. The importance of the so-called 'soft skills' includes this need for empathy and social awareness.

How do you 'read the room'? As with so many aspects of communication and collaboration, there is no panacea. You can study specialist areas deeply such as reading body language and so forth, but there are some simple steps you can take that will probably give you what you actually need. First of all – pay attention. Listen, look and digest what you see. Is it a happy room (are people laughing and smiling)? Can you detect underlying tension? Are people grouping into potential factions? All of these things can give you an indication of what's going on. An old rule of thumb I've heard used for many years is, 'You have two ears and one mouth – when in a discussion, use them in that ratio.' Talk only when you need to – because when you're talking, you can't listen.

A happy room is more likely to accept a bright, breezy presentation rather better than a dark, hostile, fractious room. There are circumstances when you may face direct hostility. It's very much more useful if you can pick up this hostility early in any engagement because it gives you the chance to address it before it escalates.

You can train yourself to become better at social awareness. There are courses and publications on body language, making positive eye-contact and using verbal techniques such as asking open questions to help engage someone. I return to my simple approach – if you know of someone who is good at reading a room, watch them, learn from them and then emulate them.

RELATIONSHIP MANAGEMENT

No human relationship, be it personal or professional, is possible without some degree of conflict. Effective EI includes the ability to use a range of techniques to prevent, manage and resolve conflict and improve the way a relationship works.

From my own professional background there is an oft-quoted metric relating to the cost of implementing a security control early on during a project, and the relative cost of retrofitting it once the project is live. It's set at 10–1. It is 10 times more expensive to retrofit a control than to implement it early. I've never seen this tested in any formal or empirical manner, but I'm sure you get the gist. The same applies to conflict. The best approach is to stop it as early as possible and avoid the inevitable collateral damage should the conflict manifest. This does not mean you don't seek to deal with the root causes of the conflict – you just need to take the emotional heat out of the equation.

At this point it's worth mentioning that not all conflict is harmful. In a healthy organisation,[76] discussion and debate (aka conflict) can be the catalyst for innovation and creativity. This section looks almost exclusively at negative conflict.

---

[76] Check out Chapter 8 where organisational health as discussed by John Cleese is considered.

Most workplace conflicts are due to conflicting priorities. These can be resource-based (people, budget, equipment and so forth), or personality-based. They're normally a cunning mixture of the two. As with many areas of EI, the first aspect to consider (seemingly paradoxically) is the reduction of emotion. When conflict is personal it tends to arouse true anger, and this in turn increases the conflict's negativity. Just as with social awareness, detecting conflict before it has become really obvious is a skill. The same approach pertains – pay attention. Listen, look and digest what you see.

The ability to detect when 'banter' has moved on into abuse or bullying is essential. This is sometimes referred to as facilitation management. The first evidence of negative, non-resolved conflict tends to be minor verbal interjections, negative body language and tone of voice. Your next step is to intervene assertively and positively. If you are in a managerial position, it's often sensible to set up a regime that exposes the conflict in a manner that limits damage and protects the self-esteem of those involved. A simple process is as follows:

1. Using a venue that could be considered 'neutral' by the participants, set up a meeting that has one agenda item – resolve the conflict.

2. You should set simple terms of reference that request that participants act in a respectful manner and that they understand they will each (or all if there are multiple parties involved) be given the chance to speak without interruption or aggression.

3. Each participant should be asked to describe their perception of the conflict without making accusatory remarks or making any personal comments about other participants. Each should be given the chance to respond to others' contribution – using the same approach to avoid being accusatory.

4. You (acting as chairperson for the session) should then provide a summary and get all parties to agree to this summary. This will be hard.

5. You then need to chair a session wherein everyone tries to set out a solution. All options are on the table, but those that are obviously impractical or unacceptable are dropped. Once you have a series of agreed potential solutions, each will need further analysis. It is unlikely this can be done in a single session, but the outlines can be described and agreed.

6. The session should then jointly agree the next steps, and this should be documented, agreed and ultimately circulated. As with all such things, actions need to be allocated with named owners, and if possible, a timeframe should also be agreed.

7. You should then close the meeting, send out the documented agreements and timescales, and continue the process in the same manner as it is a continuous cycle.

These steps can only work if your EI has kicked in at the right point to allow you to deploy the approach. The two elements need to work together. It may not resolve the entire conflict. So often what you see are symptoms rather than the root cause of the problem. If nothing else, the approach will get you closer to resolving the issue than avoiding dealing with the matter, which is often a tempting, but ultimately self-defeating option.

EI is practical and can be used across your personal and professional life. Given the fact that 'soft skills' account for 85 per cent of a person's professional effectiveness, it's hard to discount it. It can assist you solve problems that work in a collaborative manner, and help you and your teammates:

- accept positive criticism;
- learn from mistakes and not let them fester;
- say **no** when it needs to be said.

EI can lead to better relationships, improved personal and professional well-being, and help everybody develop stronger communication skills.

ROOT CAUSE ANALYSIS (RCA)

Although normally applied in technical areas such as IT, engineering and similar, the RCA approach can be applied as part of helping to resolve conflict, in that it goes beyond treating symptoms and seeks to eradicate the problem entirely. There are circumstances wherein RCA can be applied to prevent incidents before they arise, but I'll look solely at the reactive approach to help support conflict resolution.

RCA can be decomposed into four steps:

1. Clear identification and description of the problem.
2. Accurate description of the chronology of the event – from 'normal' to the event itself.
3. Clear distinction between symptoms and 'steps' within the problem and the actual root cause.
4. Graphic depiction of the route from root to event.

If you can identify the thing that – if removed – stops the problem from happening again, it's likely to be the 'root cause'. Many of the sub-issues identified are often contributory to the problem but are not the ultimate cause. Removing these sub-issues is normally a positive thing, but the action rarely prevents recurrence.

CONCLUSION

Emotional intelligence and self-knowledge provide a means to make better decisions if we understand what is important and what our strengths and weaknesses are. We can do this by setting realistic goals, building stronger relationships and generally making life more fulfilling.

This requires you to be honest with yourself, be open to feedback from all sources (however uncomfortable), being self-aware and being patient. Self-knowledge is ongoing and takes time and effort to learn who you really are. You won't have all the answers immediately. You probably will **never** have all the answers.

12 PERSONAL BRANDING

DISCLOSURE AND INTENT

One of the many themes that keeps emerging in this book is that of 'disclosure'. It is used as part of the Johari Window Model and forms one of the themes relating to assertiveness. Personal branding also touches on disclosure, but in this case, it is very deliberate, very measured and purposeful.

Personal branding has been discussed for many years, although never as much as recently. This is probably due to the impact of social media – and this includes more 'professional' platforms such as LinkedIn. In 1999, the feted management consultancy writer Tom Peters published a book, *The Brand You 50 (Reinventing Work): Fifty Ways to Transform Yourself from an 'Employee' into a Brand That Shouts Distinction, Commitment, and Passion!*[77] The concept has mushroomed and been used to great effect by people as diverse and the Kardashians, the Dalai Lama and Donald Trump.

I have to question how relevant the concept is to mainstream IT professionals. It may be that the workplace will evolve to become a marketplace for people of skill with a need to constantly seek new opportunities and placements without the embrace of what is currently a 'job'. My questioning is perhaps rooted in my own background and age – millennials, Gen-Z and whatever replaces them may have fewer doubts regarding what could be seen as overt self-promotion and aggrandisement. I will try to put my questioning to one side and outline the concept in a positive manner.

Building a personal brand may seem initially to be self-centred, but many authors and promoters of the concept suggest it is anything but. It's very much about how you present yourself to the world and what value you can bring. It is clear that most of the same authors and promoters are very keen to ensure that personal brands are honest, genuine, consistent and focused. It is this last element that is repeated constantly. A brand of any variety needs to focus on targeted audiences. Tom Spitale (former GE and Walmart marketer) wrote in Forbes magazine in September 2021[78] as follows:

> When designing new offerings, companies with a broad focus ask a variety of different customers about their needs. Typically, those needs differ greatly. So, what

---

77 Peters, T. (1999) *The Brand You 50 (Reinventing Work): Fifty Ways to Transform Yourself from an 'Employee' into a Brand That Shouts Distinction, Commitment, and Passion!* New York: Knopf.

78 Spitale, T. (2021) *How narrowing your focus can lead to more growth*. Forbes. Available from https://www.forbes.com/sites/forbesagencycouncil/2021/09/08/how-narrowing-your-focus-can-lead-to-more-growth/?sh=bcf993865a3f.

do most companies do? They 'average' the results and make products that don't please anyone.

We call this 'lukewarm tea syndrome'. Some customers like their tea hot, some like it cold, so you make something in the middle. No one likes lukewarm tea, but you made it because your focus was too wide.

You have to target your brand, and all its accompanying communications to the audience you are seeking to engage with. This may seem pretty obvious to many – if applying for a job, it makes sense to customise your CV to the specific needs of a job – highlighting the skills and experience the potential employer is advertising. In many ways, this is a small-scale example of branding. How you present yourself on social media, including LinkedIn, is essentially dressing a shop window. The temptation is, of course, to broaden the appeal of your offering as you cannot determine exactly who is going to look at your profile. Lukewarm tea strikes again... You have to craft your presence to help people understand what you stand for, what you want to focus on, and this in turn can lead to making better connections. It can improve the quality of your professional life by helping you find work and tasks that you want to do, rather than doing what you have to in a job you have had little input into moulding.

Branding needs to be backed up with genuine capability and achievement, otherwise you are building on sand. Branding is not about credibility or reputation – you have to deal with this before you start developing your brand. It is about visibility and determining what you want people to know, and to help them make the best decisions about **you**.

Reputation is different – it's the collective understanding people have of you based on their experience of you and what they hear about you. You need to manage this – and only then can you brand yourself successfully. Reputation is rarely deliberate – personal branding is intentional and therefore deliberate. It's in your control. It is how you want people to see you. Whereas reputation is about credibility, your personal brand is about visibility and the values that you outwardly represent.

HOW TO BUILD YOUR PERSONAL BRAND

It's important to note that branding is a dynamic process, not just a single event of building a brand. It has to evolve as the world changes. Brands can go toxic and fail – a series of business failures within a group of branded companies can infect even those parts that are successful. You have to manage the brand to ensure it remains clean.

Step 1: what do you want to do?

Ask the following questions:

- What skills or talent do you have that you take pride in?
- Beyond paying the bills, what gets you out of bed in the morning?
- What are you curious about professionally?
- What parts of your professional life 'rock your boat'?

- Are there any specialist areas that catch your attention?
- Do you have any heroes and how might you be like them?
- How would you like to be seen and remembered?

Whilst not following the scientific method, write your answers down and analyse them to see if there are any themes, connections and synergies between them. Whilst you may already know what your beliefs and values are, this process can help to structure them in a way that helps to focus them into something actionable. You may realise that you have a penchant for organising events in a short space of time – grabbing reluctant people into your world and energising them into helping you. I know a lot of people love a good crisis, but it's a rare skill to deal with them effectively.

One you've worked out what you like to do, and feel comfortable doing, it may be that you're in a good position to begin shaping your professional life in a way to make use of your talents. You may also learn a lot about yourself by analysing the traits of those people you admire. If you value their clarity of communication, it may behove you to consider improving your own skills in this area (you've made a good start by reading this book). Knowing what 'rocks your boat' will help you to focus on your particular and peculiar skills and capabilities and consider how you both demonstrate and communicate your newly unearthed talents.

Step 2: goal alignment

If your values and beliefs do not align with the organisation you're working for, you'll have trouble being effective. Whilst seeking to change others' values and beliefs is a perfectly legitimate aim in many circumstances, to operate when out of sync with your peers is difficult and prone to failure. It's an obvious step to look at what values and beliefs pertain to your current situation. You can look at others in the organisation to see what they value, and whether they are effective or not.

It's worth analysing what works, and then revisiting your own skills and capabilities to see how best you can fit. As with all things, there's always a need for compromise. There's never a situation when you have perfect alignment with all your peer group or your employer, and some tinkering and adjustment is perfectly understandable and normal. Just as when you adjust your CV when applying for a particular role with a particular company, you will most likely have to do the same when dealing with any organisation.

What is important is to remember that if any misalignment is so profound that you cannot realistically make an adjustment without compromising yourself morally, personally or professionally – you're are probably working for the wrong crew.

You may find that to align yourself you need to adopt or acquire new knowledge or skills. This 'gap analysis' can provide you with a very personal training needs guide. There are formal techniques referred to as training needs analysis (TNA). Goal alignment and skills gap analysis is an effective a way of performing your own very personal TNA.

If you are struggling with this approach, one simple method is to scan the organisation's documents and look for key words or phrases. Examples might include innovation, creativity, social responsibility, eco-friendly and so forth. These can be used to reflect on your personal analysis you performed in Step 1 to see how you align. Whilst many organisations have stated aims, some of them differ in reality. You cannot treat corporate publications as totally trustworthy, as they are often PR pieces rather than a statement of true intent – depicting how they want to appear rather than how they actually are.

Step 3: who are you talking to – and why?

The concept of an 'audience' for your communication is repeated throughout this book. You need to know who you need to communicate with, how and why. You need to know who needs to listen to you so you can present your brand. If you follow many of the writers on personal branding, they are clear that you need to find a niche that is specific to you. You need to deliver your message to people who care about the niche you have decided to occupy.

You can set out a mind map or similar diagram to identify your various audiences. There is rarely just one. Some are decision makers. Others are holders of knowledge and similar power. Others might be politically pivotal to your quest – without having much formal power. It's worth noting that many organisations have formal rules, regulations, policies, standards and working practices. What is very clear is that many of these are disregarded by many, and it's the informal rules and loosely based social alliances (often referred to as the 'unwritten rules'[79]) that are important. Work out who you need to talk to and why you need to talk to them, then adjust your brand in accordance with your audience.

Although there are often people who dislike being buttonholed by ambitious people pursuing their own agenda, a sound organisation should recognise when someone is trying to effect positive change, and making your intended contribution known to those in power (informal and otherwise) should be seen as a good thing. If you cannot progress because there are entrenched people who will not engage with you, and the organisation resists you, you may again be working for the wrong crew.

Step 4: engage

You now know what you want to say, how you want to say it and to whom you want to communicate. It's time to broadcast. This can be uncomfortable for many, especially if you are dealing with senior people who you've not dealt with before. The key is preparation. If you approach someone with a solution to a problem you know they're facing, you are for more likely to get their attention than simply telling people about your brilliant ideas. Too often I've heard 'bring me solutions, not problems' from senior colleagues.

You need to make sure that they know what your values and beliefs are, but there is an inevitable question they will ask – most likely internally to themselves. They will ask, 'what's in it for me?' This is similar to the 'bring me solutions' phrase above. If you offer a solution for a problem they have, and it brings them benefits (increased revenue, better time management, personal glory or great praise) you will make headway. Shouting 'look at me, I'm great' will not succeed.

---

79 One of the most effective means by which workers can put pressure on organisational management during a dispute is to 'work to rule'. Never disregard the informal.

Just as you adjust your CV when applying for a job, you should adjust your brand to meet the needs of your audience.

It's in these circumstances that the skills discussed in this book around emotional intelligence come into play. If you empathise with people, you will communicate better. If you appear genuinely interested in them and their problems, they will reciprocate by giving you airtime and attention. As with so many aspects of communication and collaboration, it is the combination of skills that matter. No single technique nor behavioural facet will push you to succeed – it's the combination that will make you effective and allow you to utilise your personal brand to the fullest.

BRAND CHARACTERISTICS

There are a range of characteristics that are very likely to make your personal brand more effective. It's not all about your personal needs and wants. The following list suggests a number of professional traits that should form part of the way you present yourself. There are a number of publications that set out behaviours that are expected from a professional. The BCS Code of Conduct is as good place to start as any.

- You need to ensure people know and understand that you have an appropriate work ethic, that you are a positive person who delivers with true passion. Some of the simplest things can make a huge difference.

- Make sure you are prepared before meetings – reading the meeting notes whilst it takes place makes you less effective and suggests you are either a poor time manager or disrespectful to the meeting organiser.

- Be on time. I know life intervenes and disrupts the best-planned day, but punctuality really helps.

- Be prepared to accept that sometimes you get things wrong. Accept there are subjects and concepts that may require you to do some research or undergo training. There is nothing wrong with saying 'I don't know' – provided you don't have to say it too often.

- Positivism is important. Whilst we should know that there are times when to say 'no', it should not be an automatic response. You have to make things happen if you can. A personal brand that includes you being a 'blocker' is pretty toxic. This characteristic – and all those listed above – can help you to develop credibility for your brand. A brand is about how you present yourself. If it isn't credible, what's the point?

- Finally – be nice. Being nasty might bring short-term results, but in time, it will crash and burn. Dictatorships always fail.

CONCLUSION

Just as with enabling your emotional intelligence, personal branding takes time and effort, but it should help you play the long game, as it can help you to achieve career goals, build meaningful relationships, and live a more fulfilling life. You need to be authentic, consistent, helpful and active. You need to engage with others to create and present your brand. They will not come to you.

13 POSITIVE ATTITUDE

A quick check on the number of times I have used the word 'positive' in this book indicates that its use is spread across many chapters, and there are over 20 instances. The word is included in phrases such as:

- positive flexible attitude;
- open, positive and empathetic body language;
- ...a fundamental human skill that if undertaken positively will enhance...;
- to intervene assertively and positively;
- corresponding positive impact;
- positive benefits.

Positivism is undoubtedly a force to be reckoned with.

THE HISTORY OF POSITIVE MENTAL ATTITUDE (PMA)

The history of the concept often referred to as a positive mental attitude is at best chequered. Most publications on the subject cite one man as being the originator of the concept. He is Napoleon Hill, a self-help author who, in 1937, published a best-selling book called *Think and Grow Rich*[80] in which he mentions the concept of PMA (but not the exact phrase). In 1959, Hill and W. Clement Stone co-authored and published another book called *Success Through a Positive Mental Attitude*.[81]

Hill's claims and personal backstory indicate clearly that he was a conman, a misogynist and a criminal. His book sold millions, and it remains highly influential. What is also clear is that a PMA cannot of itself cure cancer, provide you with commercial success nor make you rich. But it helps.

Research undertaken in 2018[82] shows that there is a neurological link between PMA and improved learning amongst schoolchildren. The research was the first study to

---

80 Hill, N. (1937) *Think and Grow Rich*. Meriden, CT: The Ralston Society.

81 Hill, N. and Stone, W.C. (1959) *Success Through a Positive Mental Attitude*. New York: Pocket Books.

82 Chen, L., Bae, S.R., Battista, C., Qin, S., Chen, T., Evans, T.M. and Menon, V. (2018) Positive attitude toward math supports early academic success: behavioral evidence and neurocognitive mechanisms. *Psychological Science*, 29 (3). 390–402.

reveal neural mechanisms that link PMA with actual achievement. PMA increased the effectiveness of the children's learning and memory abilities and resulted in improved academic success.

Despite his flaws, it seems that Napoleon Hill may have been right – perhaps inadvertently. Despite the above referenced research, there is little true understanding as to how PMA works. The Mayo Clinic in the USA is emphatic in its support. Its website states:[83]

> Researchers continue to explore the effects of positive thinking and optimism on health. Health benefits that positive thinking **may** provide include:
>
> - Increased life span
> - Lower rates of depression
> - Lower levels of distress and pain
> - Greater resistance to illnesses
> - Better psychological and physical well-being
> - Better cardiovascular health and reduced risk of death from cardiovascular disease and stroke
> - Reduced risk of death from cancer
> - Reduced risk of death from respiratory conditions
> - Reduced risk of death from infections
> - Better coping skills during hardships and times of stress
>
> It's unclear why people who engage in positive thinking experience these health benefits. One theory is that having a positive outlook enables you to cope better with stressful situations, which reduces the harmful health effects of stress on your body.
>
> It's also thought that positive and optimistic people tend to live healthier lifestyles — they get more physical activity, follow a healthier diet, and don't smoke or drink alcohol in excess.

It's notable that the Mayo Clinic uses the expression 'benefits that positive thinking **may** provide include...' The jury is still out on this. However, although not backed by a large amount of empirical research, all the apocryphal evidence supports the Mayo Clinic statement. PMA makes your life better and improves the lives of those around you. Whilst blindly hoping for the best is not often a good strategy, rational, action-oriented thinking will take you further than acting like Eeyore.

---

83 https://www.mayoclinic.org/healthy-lifestyle/stress-management/in-depth/positive-thinking/art-20043950.

'CAN-DO' AND FAITH

I think that PMA relates closely to a 'can-do' attitude. Constantly looking for solutions is the best approach to getting things done, no matter how annoying you might be when doing it. It's about not giving up, looking for alternative ways of achieving things and avoiding feeling hopeless or helpless. PMA also provides a means to do things quickly and suggests either bravery or a lack of fear. It also suggests an attitude that alludes more to faith than linear, logical, rational thinking. Just as in many faith-based philosophies such as monotheistic religions, maybe we're not meant to know why it works. With that in mind, I will return to the works of the serial bankrupt, misogynist conman, Napoleon Hill. In *Think and Grow Rich*, he set out 13 principles:[84]

1. Desire: Start with a strong desire or burning ambition to achieve a specific goal or outcome.

2. **Faith**: Have unwavering faith in yourself and your ability to achieve your goal.

3. Autosuggestion: Use positive self-talk and affirmations to reinforce your beliefs and goals.

4. Specialized knowledge: Acquire the knowledge and skills needed to achieve your goal.

5. Imagination: Use your imagination to visualize your goal and see yourself achieving it.

6. Organized planning: Develop a detailed plan of action to achieve your goal.

7. Decision: Make a firm decision to follow through on your plan and never give up.

8. Persistence: Keep working towards your goal, even when faced with obstacles or setbacks.

9. **Power of the Master Mind**: Surround yourself with like-minded people who support and encourage you.

10. **The Mystery of Sex Transmutation**: Use the power of your sexual energy to fuel your desire and drive.

11. The Subconscious Mind: Tap into the power of your subconscious mind to help you achieve your goals.

12. The Brain: Use your brain to analyze and plan, and to make decisions and take action.

13. **The Sixth Sense**: Trust your intuition and inner guidance to help you make the right decisions and achieve your goals.

I've emboldened some words and phrases that are indicators of Hill's other interests – he and one of his many wives were connected to The Royal Fraternity of the Master Metaphysicians, a cult led by a man called James Bernard Schafer. The Fraternity considered *Think and Grow Rich* to be a religious tract. Schafer tried to make a child in his care immortal.

---

84 Hill, N. (1937) *Think and Grow Rich*. Meriden, CT: The Ralston Society.

If we disregard these strange elements, Hill's list strikes me as being very positive (there you go – I've said 'positive' again). If we draw out the appropriate phrases, the list does become useful. The phrases are:

- Develop a detailed plan of action.
- Keep working towards your goal – be persistent.
- Make firm decisions.
- Acquire specialist knowledge.

Just as personal branding requires focus and ensuring you find an appropriate niche, acquiring specialist knowledge seems to be an essential part of pursuing a PMA. Firmness, decisiveness, persistence and being action-oriented take this forward. Faith and self-belief complete this picture. Napoleon Hill might have been a charlatan, but he was pretty good at delivering a pithy list of sensible things to do.

HOW TO DEVELOP AND MAINTAIN A PMA

Moving away from the messier end of self-help, I have trawled the literature and the web looking for tips and hints on how to develop and maintain a PMA. There are a multitude of '10 ways to develop a PMA', '15 tips on getting positive', 'How to get rid of the negative people in your life'. Everyone's an expert, a life coach or a pop psychologist. Napoleon Hill has created a raft of charlatans. So – I did the only thing I could. I looked at all the lists of hints, tips, advice and bon mots and distilled them into something that looks like sense. It's a bit like going through Hill's principles and arriving at useful phrases.

DISTILLED POSITIVITY

- Look for the positive. It's easy to fall into the trap of 'catastrophising' and only seeing the worst case. The worst case rarely happens.
- Work out the things that you should be grateful for – health, family, friends and Scotland winning at Twickenham.
- Laugh. Most things are ridiculous in the final analysis.
- Mix with happy people and avoid the doom-mongers, nay-sayers and Cassandras.
- Don't be so hard on yourself. It's, 'I'll do it better next time' rather than, 'Wow – I messed that up' – unless you laugh loudly at your messing up. Remember – comedy = tragedy + time.
- Every mistake is a chance to remember to not do it again.
- Every now and then you **must** tell your critical inner voice to shut up.
- Stop comparing yourself to others – we're all good and bad at different things.
- Take a break – switch off the phone. You're not that important. Stop and smell the roses.

- Think long term – are you going to worry about the stressful thing that's bothering you now in two years' time? I didn't think so.

- Remember that there are things you can change – and things you can't. Focus on the possible.

- Listen to uplifting music. Not The Smiths. Nor The Verve.

- Seek help when you need it. Don't leave it too late. People are often pleased to be able to help. You can't do everything.

- Face your problems. Hiding them doesn't work. Drag them out, deal with them and you'll feel better immediately.

- Live in the moment – the future is what it will be. Mindfulness is a silly word but the concept is sound.

- Learn to say 'no'. Once you get used to it it's great fun.

- Be nice.

CONCLUSION

If you are positive, and you communicate positivity, you will pass it on to others. It is truly infectious, just like a laugh. Collaboration goes better when people are engaged and positive. Even if the apocryphal is not true, and PMA is not the panacea many suggest it is, PMA will make work a nicer place, and you will have a better time – both at work and at home.

14 NETWORKING

There are two types of networking that relate to collaboration. One involves the development of a network of external people with whom you connect – primarily to establish business connections to facilitate sales and marketing, although it can also involve technical discussion and sharing. The other is more internally focused, in that you often have to develop a network of internal connections within your own organisation in order to get things done.

I'll start with the latter. In many organisations you need to know, amongst many other things, how to:

- establish a project budget;
- convince a board member to invest in your brilliant idea;
- get hold of a work code to complete your timesheet;
- obtain information on a specialist technical area;
- claim travelling expenses;
- how to make a complaint to HR.

There are many things that you only have to do occasionally, and there's nothing like having a colleague who knows how to do them. There are so many people I refer to as my 'go-tos' who help me do specialist things easily and quickly. An important aspect of having go-tos is knowing when you have to ask, 'who knows how to do X?' Once you find out who they are, and they are useful, they become another of your go-tos.

You can't do everything yourself – one of the reasons why we have teams is that the combination of skills a team offers makes it effective – greater perhaps than the sum of its parts.

I refer back to an occasion when a school friend was trying to join the Royal Marines. This involved a series of interviews followed by an intensive series of tests held somewhere remote, cold and horrible. He passed the Officer Selection interviews and ended up commanding a team that was tasked with carrying a very heavy barrel across an imaginary chasm using ropes, planks and similar. Each of the people commanding these tasks were given a real, live Royal Marine to assist in the team. The final act was to carry the heavy barrel across the chasm using whatever bridge or similar they had devised as part of the test. All the other candidates carried the barrel themselves – some toppling into the chasm. My school friend looked at the barrel, and then looked at the very large Royal Marine who had been seconded into his team. He simply asked him to carry the barrel – no point in breaking your back when you have a beast of a man to do the job. He was the only person who was selected from his cohort of candidates.

The lesson is simple – don't always do it yourself.

We have already looked at the use of the term 'what's in it for me?' in relation to persuading people to do things for you. You have to empathise with others. You have to use this technique when networking, because everyone is there for a reason, and it **won't** be to help you out. As in all exchanges, networking events are opportunities to agree bargains with people to mutual advantage. You have to be able to understand what they want in order to get what you want. You also need to understand the need for compromise. You need to convince people of the value you bring to them before you can start getting value **from** them.

CONCLUSION

The parallels between enabling emotional intelligence, personal branding and professional networking are significant. To maximise your effectiveness regarding professional networking you need to follow the same basic truths:

- Be prepared. Take time before a networking event to consider what you want to say and to whom you want to speak.
- Be consistent.
- Be genuine. Play acting will get spotted pretty quickly.
- Be interested in others. Ask questions and actually listen to the answers.
- Be nice.

15 SUMMARY AND CONCLUSION

Digital, people, business and skills. These were the most prominent four words that emerged from a Word Cloud I create from the text of this book (Figure 15.1).

Figure 15.1 Word cloud

It's perhaps not surprising that the word 'collaboration' is prominent and 'communication' occurs twice, but the four key words stand out – digital, people, business and skills. The combination of these elements is the key to delivering a successful organisation, and at the heart of all this is communication and collaboration.

One of the joys of writing a book such as this is the necessity to do some research. This can take you down many roads and alleys – some of them blind – but there are always some nuggets of great beauty and joy. One such nugget is a booklet distributed by the US Office of Strategic Services to would-be saboteurs in Nazi-occupied territories. The purpose of the booklet was to 'characterize simple sabotage, to outline its possible effects, and to present suggestions for inciting and executing it'.[85] One section caught

---

85 Office of Strategic Services (1944) *Simple Sabotage Field Manual*. Washington DC: Director of Strategic Services: Office of Strategic Services.

my eye. It had a series of instructions on how to disrupt an organisation from within by simple means in a section entitled, 'General Interference with Organizations and Production'. I was given the document because a colleague suggested that many of the acts of sabotage recommended in the book were in fact common practice in the organisation we were then working in. I was struck by how many of these recommended acts related to communication and collaboration. I'll list a few examples:

- Insist on doing everything through 'channels'. Never permit short-cuts to be taken in order to expedite decisions.

- When possible, refer all matters to committees, for 'further study and consideration'. Attempt to make the committees as large as possible—never less than five.

- Haggle over precise wordings of communications, minutes, resolutions.

- Refer back to matters decided upon at the last meeting and attempt to re-open the question of the advisability of that decision.

- Be worried about the propriety of any decision—raise the question of whether such action as is contemplated lies within the jurisdiction of the group or whether it might conflict with the policy of some higher echelon.

- 'Misunderstand' orders. Ask endless questions or engage in long correspondence about such orders. Quibble over them when you can.

- When training new workers, give incomplete or misleading instructions.

- Prolong correspondence with government bureaus.

- Pretend that instructions are hard to understand, and ask to have them repeated more than once. Or pretend that you are particularly anxious to do your work, and pester the foreman with unnecessary questions.

- Give lengthy and incomprehensible explanations when questioned.

- Do not cooperate in salvage schemes.

It strikes me that each of the above is the antithesis of what I've tried to outline in this book. Whilst sabotage is a strong and emotive word, there's no doubt that interrupting information flows can have the same effect. Unhealthy organisations tend to be unsuccessful, and the key to corporate health seems to be clear communications that enable positive collaboration. An unhealthy organisation can be considered 'self-sabotaging'. Part of our role is to find a way to stop this, or at least, minimise its impact. Self-sabotage is a syndrome that can apply as easily to people as to organisations, and many of the suggested means I found during research that should help people overcome the self-sabotage syndrome echo many of the themes outlined in this book. One theme relates to positivity. Others relate to self-awareness and assertiveness. I have no doubt that the practices suggested in this book are to help organisations help themselves – which is very much part of the IT business partner's role.

Further to this conclusion is the fact that most of the ways we can best support the organisations we serve are little to do with technology, and almost exclusively to do with how we treat people. Practicing active listening, empathy and self-awareness are very human things, and perhaps boil down to a simple instruction – 'be nice'. Aggression, blame-shifting, impossible deadlines and lack of empathy are a recipe for failure.

Assertion need not be sugar-sweet and can challenge some people, but it is lightyears ahead of directed, negative personalised criticism.

A further conclusion is that there is an ongoing need for awareness – personal and organisational. I talked earlier about the 'paradox' of communication, in that you have to present information that is truly informative – without patronising parts of your audience or readership. You have to be aware of who you're talking to, what they actually want, what their own particular skills and experience are and why you're talking to them. There should always be, to a greater or lesser degree, a purpose to your communication. You have to seek balance at all times, and the key to achieving this is awareness.

A final thought – there are normally consequences to collaboration and communication failure. Most of the time they are relatively minor – financial loss and similar. However, there are occasions where things can get really serious. The 1986 Space Shuttle disaster could have been prevented if decision makers had acted upon concerns presented by engineers regarding the safety of the launch vehicle in very cold conditions. It's possible that the loss of the submersible Titan in 2023 was related to a similar communication failure. In both cases, the people raising the concerns were not retained by the organisations involved – perhaps as a result of raising the concerns. Assertiveness and active listening may have helped prevent such events. Even safety-critical components can be compromised by poor communications – especially when there are external forces like cost pressures at work. The degradation of building safety standards is evidenced by the Grenfell Tower disaster in 2017. Clearer communications could have ensured that standards were maintained rather than circumvented. This communications and collaboration stuff matters – it can make the difference between life and death.

APPENDIX

CARNEGIE FOUNDATION – A STUDY OF ENGINEERING EDUCATION

Figure A.1 Charles Riborg Mann's *A Study of Engineering Education*

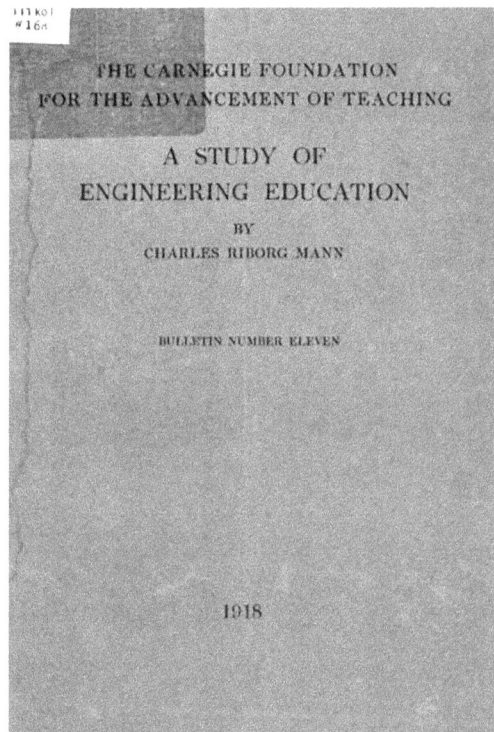

Charles Riborg Mann published *A Study of Engineering Education*, prepared for the Joint Commission of Engineering Education societies. One of the core requirements of the study was to analyse the educational and training requirements of the engineering profession as a whole. The report states:

> At the first meeting of the Joint Committee of the National Engineering Societies with representatives of the Carnegie Foundation for the Advancement of Teaching it was agreed that an analysis of the requirements of the engineering profession was one of the first essential steps in this study of technological education. Accordingly

a number of representative engineers were questioned in personal interviews concerning the factors that are most powerful in determining success in engineering work and most effective in building up the engineering profession. These interviews, together with a study of the methods of rating college graduates in several large manufacturing companies, indicated that personal qualities such as common sense, integrity, resourcefulness, initiative, tact, thoroughness, accuracy, efficiency, and understanding of men are universally recognized as being no less necessary to a professional engineer than are technical knowledge and skill.

The report continues:

The statement that individuality counts for as much as learning for the engineer, just as it does for the lawyer or the physician, seems like a veritable platitude. Yet because the engineering schools have always made it their chief aim to impart the technical information needed in industrial production, and because both scientific knowledge and industrial practice have grown so rapidly, the attention of technical schools has been focused chiefly on keeping up to date in science and practice. The university emphasis on research in natural science has also tended to magnify the importance of technique and to minimize the importance of personality; until curricula have become so congested with specialized courses that students generally regard literature and sociology as unnecessary chores, to be endured rather than enjoyed. Therefore it seemed necessary to consider the question whether this emphasis on technique is producing a new and higher type of engineer, or whether the engineering profession still stakes its faith on the fundamental thesis that personal character is, after all, the real foundation for achievement.

Some 1,500 engineers responded to an approach that asked them to state whether technical engineering knowledge was more important that personal characteristics. The responses revealed that personal characteristics were identified seven times more than technical knowledge as being more important for an engineer to be successful. The results are clear – technical knowledge accounts for some 15 per cent in regard to an engineer being successful. Personal characteristics account for 85 per cent.

A subsequent study based on this research was sent to many thousands of engineers from the ranks of a number of professional bodies. The study requested respondents to prioritise six aspects of a person's personal characteristics to determine which of these would be most important in helping an engineer be successful. The six aspects were:

- character;
- judgement;
- efficiency;
- understanding of men;
- knowledge;
- technique.

More than 7,000 engineers responded and 94.5 per cent placed 'character' at the top. 'Technique' came last.

The report states:

> This definition of the essential characteristics of the professional engineer is important, because it proves that in spite of the enormous development of scientific information and technical skill, the engineers of America have not been beguiled into thinking that efficient control of the forces of nature is the sole requirement for achievement in applied science. Therefore the schools that intend to train engineers cannot afford to neglect wholly the personalities of the students. While it is obvious that personal traits like integrity, initiative, and common sense cannot be taught didactically like the rule of three, it is no less obvious that the growth of these essential characteristics in students may be either fostered and encouraged or inhibited and discouraged by the manner in which the school is organized and the subject-matter presented. The problems of finding the best organization, of constructing the best curriculum, and of discovering the best methods of teaching cannot be solved by logic alone or by research in natural science.

It is clear that the 'soft skills' are of paramount importance. Mann notes that many human characteristics can be taught didactically, but they need to be nurtured and encouraged. The role of such things as professional codes of conduct provide support for this approach. As Mann says – they need to be 'fostered and encouraged or inhibited and discouraged' as necessary.

UNITED STATES. OFFICE OF STRATEGIC SERVICES. SIMPLE SABOTAGE FIELD MANUAL

The text below is an extract from the OSS *Simple Sabotage Field Manual*.[86] The items listed are designed for saboteurs working in management of administrative positions in enemy organisations.

General Interference with Organizations and Production

(a) Organizations and Conferences

(1) Insist on doing everything through "channels." Never permit short-cuts to be taken in order to expedite decisions.

(2) Make "speeches." Talk as frequently as possible and at great length. Illustrate your "points" by long anecdotes and accounts of personal experiences. Never hesitate to make a few appropriate "patriotic" comments.

(3) When possible, refer all matters to committees, for "further study and consideration." Attempt to make the committees as large as possible—never less than five.

(4) Bring up irrelevant issues as frequently as possible.

(5) Haggle over precise wordings of communications, minutes, resolutions.

---

[86] Office of Strategic Services (1944) *Simple Sabotage Field Manual*. Washington DC Director of Strategic Services: Office of Strategic Services.

(6) Refer back to matters decided upon at the last meeting and attempt to re-open the question of the advisability of that decision.

(7) Advocate "caution." Be "reasonable" and urge your fellow-conferees to be "reasonable" and avoid haste which might result in embarrassments or difficulties later on.

(8) Be worried about the propriety of any decision—raise the question of whether such action as is contemplated lies within the jurisdiction of the group or whether it might conflict with the policy of some higher echelon.

(b) Managers and Supervisors

(1) Demand written orders.

(2) "Misunderstand" orders. Ask endless questions or engage in long correspondence about such orders. Quibble over them when you can.

(3) Do everything possible to delay the delivery of orders. Even though parts of an order may be ready beforehand, don't deliver it until it is completely ready.

(4) Don't order new working materials until your current stocks have been virtually exhausted, so that the slightest delay in filling your order will mean a shutdown.

(5) Order high-quality materials which are hard to get. If you don't get them argue about it. Warn that inferior materials will mean inferior work.

(6) In making work assignments, always sign out the unimportant jobs first. See that the important jobs are assigned to inefficient workers of poor machines.

(7) Insist on perfect work in relatively unimportant products; send back for refinishing those which have the least flaw. Approve other defective parts whose flaws are not visible to the naked eye.

(8) Make mistakes in routing so that parts and materials will be sent to the wrong place in the plant.

(9) When training new workers, give incomplete or misleading instructions.

(10) To lower morale and with it, production, be pleasant to inefficient workers; give them undeserved promotions. Discriminate against efficient workers; complain unjustly about their work.

(11) Hold conferences when there is more critical work to be done.

(12) Multiply paper work in plausible ways. Start duplicate files.

(13) Multiply the procedures and clearances involved in issuing instructions, pay checks, and so on. See that three people have to approve everything where one would do.

(14) Apply all regulations to the last letter.

(c) Office Workers

(1) Make mistakes in quantities of material when you are copying orders. Confuse similar names. Use wrong addresses.

(2) Prolong correspondence with government bureaus.

(3) Misfile essential documents.

(4) In making carbon copies, make one too few, so that an extra copying job will have to be done.

(5) Tell important callers the boss is busy or talking on another telephone.

(6) Hold up mail until the next collection.

(7) Spread disturbing rumors that sound like inside dope.

(d) Employees

(1) Work slowly. Think out ways to increase the number of movements necessary on your job: use a light hammer instead of a heavy one, try to make a small wrench do when a big one is necessary, use little force where considerable force is needed, and so on.

(2) Contrive as many interruptions to your work as you can: when changing the material on which you are working, as you would on a lathe or punch, take needless time to do it. If you are cutting, shaping or doing other measured work, measure dimensions twice as often as you need to. When you go to the lavatory, spend a longer time there than is necessary. Forget tools so that you will have to go back after them.

(3) Even if you understand the language, pretend not to understand instructions in a foreign tongue.

(4) Pretend that instructions are hard to understand, and ask to have them repeated more than once. Or pretend that you are particularly anxious to do your work, and pester the foreman with unnecessary questions.

(5) Do your work poorly and blame it on bad tools, machinery, or equipment. Complain that these things are preventing you from doing your job right.

(6) Never pass on your skill and experience to a new or less skilful worker.

(7) Snarl up administration in every possible way. Fill out forms illegibly so that they will have to be done over; make mistakes or omit requested information in forms.

(8) If possible, join or help organize a group for presenting employee problems to the management. See that the procedures adopted are as inconvenient as possible for the management, involving the presence of a large number of employees at each presentation, entailing more than one meeting for each grievance, bringing up problems which are largely imaginary, and so on.

(9) Misroute materials.

(10) Mix good parts with unusable scrap and rejected parts.

(12) General Devices for Lowering Morale and Creating Confusion

(a) Give lengthy and incomprehensible explanations when questioned.

(b) Report imaginary spies or danger to the Gestapo or police.

(c) Act stupid.

(d) Be as irritable and quarrelsome as possible without getting yourself into trouble.

(e) Misunderstand all sorts of regulations concerning such matters as rationing, transportation, traffic regulations.

(f) Complain against ersatz materials.

(g) In public treat axis nationals or quislings coldly.

(h) Stop all conversation when axis nationals or quislings enter a cafe.

(i) Cry and sob hysterically at every occasion, especially when confronted by government clerks.

(j) Boycott all movies, entertainments, concerts, newspapers which are in any way connected with the quisling authorities.

(k) Do not cooperate in salvage schemes.

BIBLIOGRAPHY

Bernstein, P.L. (1996) *Against the Gods – The Remarkable Story of Risk*. New York: John Wiley.

Dixon, N.F. (1979) *On the Psychology of Military Incompetence*. London: Jonathon Cape.

Dixon, N.F. (1987) *Our Own Worst Enemy*. London: Jonathon Cape.

Drucker, P. (1954) *The Practice of Management*. New York: Harper & Row.

Machiavelli, N. di B. dei (1532) *The Prince*.

McGregor, D. (1960) *The Human Side of Enterprise*. New York: McGraw Hill.

Paulos, J.A. (1988) *Innumeracy*. London: Penguin.

Peters, T. and Waterman, R.H. Jr. (1982) *In Search of Excellence*. New York: Harper & Row.

Sandman, P. https://www.psandman.com/.

Skynner, R. and Cleese, J. (1993) *LIFE and How to Survive It*. London: Methuen.

Snow, J. (1849) *On the Mode of Communication of Cholera*. London: John Churchill.

Townsend, R. (1970) *Up the Organization: How to Stop the Corporation from Stifling People and Strangling Profits*. New York: Knopf.

Xenophon (2001) *The Education of Cyrus*, 1st ed. Translated by W. Ambler. Ithaca, NY: Cornell University Press.

INDEX

www.ingramcontent.com/pod-product-compliance
Lightning Source LLC
Chambersburg PA
CBHW042032220326
41599CB00044BA/7232